MANHOOD AND PATRIOTIC AWAKENING IN THE AMERICAN CIVIL WAR

The John E. Mattoon Letters, 1859–1866

Robert Bruce Donald

Hamilton Books
A member of
The Rowman & Littlefield Publishing Group
Lanham · Boulder · New York · Toronto · Plymouth, UK

Copyright © 2008 by
Hamilton Books
4501 Forbes Boulevard
Suite 200
Lanham, Maryland 20706
Hamilton Books Acquisitions Department (301) 459-3366

Estover Road
Plymouth PL6 7PY
United Kingdom

Library of Congress Control Number: 2007937648
ISBN-13: 978-0-7618-3933-0 (paperback : alk. paper)
ISBN-10: 0-7618-3933-X (paperback : alk. paper)

Cover art, top: John E. Mattoon, January 1864. Note the stern expression and the photographer's props of shell jacket, unmarked forage cap and pistol. Collection of the author; *bottom*: John E. Mattoon on his way to an encampment of the Grand Army of the Republic, c.a. 1915. Collection of the author.

For my sons,
James A. and William H. B. Donald

TABLE OF CONTENTS

Chapter Four

Chapter Five

Chapter Six

PREFACE

My maternal great-great-grandfather John Elbert Mattoon participated in the Civil War and subsequently served in Kansas and Colorado with the 21st New York Regiment of Cavalry "Griswold Light Cavalry", under Col. William B. Tibbits. John was born on March 31, 1846. He lived a very full life passing away on December 23, 1918, a proud veteran and officer of the Grand Army of the Republic.

He enlisted at Troy, New York, on January 4, 1864. At the time he was a seventeen-year-old farmer from the tiny farming community of Canaan, New York, on the border with Massachusetts. He picked his regiment well as his Colonel and many of the officers along with a nucleus of men were experienced veterans from the 2nd New York Infantry. John Mattoon fought in a number of the major engagements in the Shenandoah Valley (Virginia and West Virginia) from March, 1864 to the end of the Civil War. He had his horse shot out from under him at the battle of New Market, on May 15, 1864. But for John Mattoon, the War had a highly unusual ending. John's unit was not disbanded at the end of the war, but was selected for duty in "Indian Territory" instead of being rapidly mustered out of service like the great majority of the hundreds of thousands of men who had fought for the Union. He was eventually dispatched to the newly founded (and short-lived) Fort Collins in Colorado Territory and assigned to guard the northern stretches of the Overland Stage route. John Mattoon was finally mustered out as a private at Denver City, Colorado Territory, on August 31, 1866. The 21st New York Cavalry became the very last Civil War volunteer cavalry regiment on active duty. He left Colorado just in time to miss the sudden surge in violence marked by Red Cloud's War and the Fetterman Massacre only a few months later. Mattoon subsequently married Anna Margaret Haight, the sister of friend, employer and brother-in-law Charley Haight, on June 2, 1867 and resided at Canaan Four Corners, NY. John and Anna had nine children including my great-grandmother Anna Margaret "Gammie" Coleman, (1883–1976). She and her only child, my grandmother,

Anna Margaret Collins (1911–1982) outlived my mother, Diana Margaret Collins Donald, (1934–1975).

Along with my sister, I came into possession of thirty eight letters faithfully held by my father, written from Joh 's late childhood up to the end of his military service in 1866. One letter i the collection is from John's brother Charley to John.

The letters have been transcribed keeping all spelling and grammatical errors intact, but I have added punctuation and capitalization in an effort to improve readability and meaning. John's experience in the Civil War was like that of many other common soldiers, but not many of those men, the great majority of them volunteers, wrote about their experiences as colorfully as John Mattoon. For this reason, I think his letters are particularly valuable for illustrating the lives and characters of the ordinary men who filled the ranks of the volunteer Union Army. Too many of the published accounts have come from the ranks of the Officer Corps. The enlisted man had different reasons for being in the war. On the positive side, there were certain financial enticements, but there were also cruel conditions and a high casualty rate, with much less glory to be shared amongst privates. Men like my great-great-grandfather had to possess enormous amounts of physical and mental toughness as well as stoic courage and steadfast loyalty to their regiment if they wanted to persevere.

Throughout the following pages I have tried to take a properly objective stance on work that pertains to a personal relation. I suspect I may have not have succeeded at times and beg your indulgence. I wish to thank my family and friends for their support, to Ronnie McNamara for her editing skill, John C. Bonnell, Jr. for his comments, and Professor Eugene E. Leach at Trinity College (Hartford) for his many and varied contributions which are deeply appreciated.

Avon, Connecticut
July 21, 2007

•

Family Members in the *John E. Mattoon Letters*

Father   William Smith Mattoon
Born: Feb. 5, 1807, the second of six children; married Sept. 24, 1825; died: Oct. 14, 1865. The family resided in Canaan, NY, then Fall River and Woodstock, NY.

Mother   Margaret Short
Born: June 6, 1811; died: Aug. 17, 1876

Sister   Harriet Elizabeth Mattoon
Born: Saugerties, NY, July 20, 1831; died: Aug. 6, 1834.

Sister   Mary Helen Mattoon Fitch
Born: Canaan, NY. Sept. 3, 1834; married Milton Fitch. Children: Mary and Julia.

Sister   Sarah "Jane" Mattoon Haight
Born: Canaan, NY. Nov. 5, 1836; married Charles [the other "Charley"] Haight of New Lebanon, NY, On Nov. 20, 1857. One child: Minnie C. Haight.

Brother   George Washington Mattoon
Born: Feb. 3, 1839; died: Mar. 15, 1871. The eldest Mattoon brother, he left for Canada in the early years of the war and then bought his way out of service. Married Mary Patton, children: Charles W. (b. Feb 3, 1863) and Herbert G.

Brother   Charles "Charley" Baldwin Mattoon

Born: Apr. 14, 1841. Served with the 5th Connecticut Infantry, Co. G, from July 10, 1861. Charley fought for four years in such battles as Cedar Mountain, VA, Chancellorsville, and on Culp's Hill at Gettysburg. On July 19, 1865 the Fifth Regiment of Veteran Volunteers was mustered out. Charley married Alice West and moved to Frederick MD, they had seven children.

Sister   Charlotte "Lot" Salisbury Mattoon Bristol
Born: Oct. 3 1843; died: 1923. Married Horace Crocker Bristol on Dec. 22, 1858. Children: Sarah Claudia born Feb. 24, 1863; then six more: Laura, Alice, Eliphlet, Clarence, Abel and Harold.

John   John Elbert Mattoon
Born: Mar. 31, 1846; died: Dec. 23, 1918. John is buried in Canaan Cemetery in the town of Canaan, Columbia County, NY. "West half of lot #1; Plot #12". He married Anna Haight (Charley Haight's sister) on June 2, 1867, and was a lifelong member of the Grand Army of the Republic, Gen. Logan Post No. 539, Chatham, NY. Anna lived to 93 (born: 1847; died: May, 1940). Her funeral was held in Chatham, NY and cost $232.

Sister   Annie Elizabeth Mattoon Stone
Born: May 27, 1848. Married Edward Huyck Stone II. Two children: Jennie May and Ruby.

Brother   Leonard "Len" Warner Mattoon.
The baby of the family, "Len" was born on June 12, 1851 and died on August 2, 1892.

Cousin   John "John Hen" Henry Mattoon
Enlisted with John E. on the same day and fought in the *same Company*. John Hen was the son of John's uncle Ben and was one of 11 children. He was born on Nov. 9, 1841. He married Jennie Foote in November of 1861 before he left for the war. He was marked "discharged" from the Regiment on June 20, 1865. "John Hen" Mattoon died on June 10, 1915.

Cousin   Thaddeus "Thad" H. Mattoon
A resident of Canaan, Thad was another son of Uncle Benjamin (born: Oct.18, 1809, died: Nov. 1, 1871). Thad was

born on June 29, 1843, and died on Feb. 22, 1908. He enlisted on August 6, 1862 in the New York 128th Regiment, Co. A, and was discharged July, 12, 1865.

Cousin   Benjamin Francis "Frank" Mattoon. Another son of Uncle Ben, enlisted in October of 1862 and served with the NY 159th Regt., Co. G. Subject of the AWOL "visit" from John in August, 1864. The 159th was finally mustered out at Augusta, Georgia, Oct. 12, 1865.

CHAPTER ONE

By sanctified tradition, the Civil War soldier who wore the Union blue was an uncomplex person who could be described adequately in a very few words . . . actually of course the man was infinitely various.

Bruce Catton[1]

This is the story of Private John E. Mattoon and his personal journey from teenage farm laborer to conflicted cavalry volunteer and finally to dedicated, patriotic Union soldier. Primary documents are the basis of this story and most particularly the previously unpublished *John E. Mattoon Letters* with many secondary works provide background information, particularly the two fine books on the 21st New York Cavalry by John C. Bonnell, Jr. and Thomas J. Reed.

In the course of the American Civil War many men shirked their duty or deserted. But many also stayed the course. Historians have pointed out that the early volunteers in the war were more emotionally and morally engaged in the conflict than their comrades who joined up later. The experiences of John Mattoon and his personal odyssey with the 21st New York Cavalry add more substance and nuance to that assertion and lay the groundwork for new and different observations.

I.   Early Life

As the rudimentarily educated third son of a farmer in 1850s New York State, John had limited opportunities. Being third-to-last son in a large family, he could not expect to inherit the family property or receive in adulthood any support from his father beyond what a common farm laborer might get. Thus he left the farm to seek employment before his thirteenth birthday. There is some evidence that he was forced to leave, as it is unlikely that he would have left his family on his own. His employers were three unmarried ladies who lived on a large farm in Wethersfield, Connecticut. When John arrived in 1859 Cordelia Harris was forty years old, Mary H. Wolcott was forty two, and Martha Blinn was aged about fifty. Martha Blinn was certainly a daughter of the large Blinn clan residing at the time in John's home town of Canaan, NY.[2] Another possible connection is that Albert N. Blinn of Canaan served in the same regiment as John's older brother Charley.[3] In any event, these employers were known to the Mattoons, and that connection certainly provided a reasonable level of comfort for John and his family. Together the widowed sisters operated one of the larger farming properties in town. Federal Census data for 1860 shows the ladies with $10,000 in real estate value and $1,000 in personal property. Additionally the 1860 Census data shows a "John Mattoon, Farm Laborer", along with one other laborer, Franklin De Wolfe, as household members. The 1870 Census lists the farm as increasing in value, being worth $12,000 along with property of $4,000.[4]

John Mattoon's situation was not at all uncommon for the time, and it appears that the three women ended up being good employers. Nonetheless, it took some intestinal fortitude to leave home at thirteen years of age, and the three letters from the period indicate that he was often asked if he was homesick. It should be noted that there was some strain or distance in John's relationship with his parents, particularly his father. Being forced to leave home at an early age may very well have had this effect. This first letter in the collection is the only one addressed to either parent. He later lamented during the war that he never heard from them. In a letter from a "Camp near Winchester" dated January 15, 1865 he wrote: "I guess the folks at home have forgotten that there is such a human being on earth as John E Mattoon and I have got so that I don't expect any letter from home any more." And later in a letter to Annie in March, "I have made up my mind to not write home anymore. They don't answer my letters and that is as good as an invitation to stop writing."[5] In fact, upon his father's death in 1865, writing from Colorado he stated: "I had not had a letter from home in so long that that I expected bad news."[6]

[Not dated; around April, 1859]

My dear Mother, I now take my pen in hand to write you a few lines to let you know that I arrived here safe and sound as a book. One of my guardians' names is Harris and I don't know the name of the other two. I don't know what the other two is. Thare is three instead to two. I do not state what day of the month it is for I don't know. I like the city of Wethersfield [CT] very much indeed. I had to wait about ten minutes after I got to Hartford, Father told Mr. Chapins to see that I got on the wright train to Hartford but he did not. When I got to Springfield I inquired whare the ticket office was and they told me, then I inquired what train was a goin to Hartford and I got on and got there safe at last. It took from 7 o'clock to three. I am not home sick yet and I hope that I shan't be. It is getting late and I must go to bed, Your son,

J E Mattoon

During a long day of travel John had the presence of mind to make sure that he got where he needed to go. Already he was exhibiting a stoicism that never left him.

May the 16th 1859

My dear Brother, I received your letter and was glad that you was all well at home. I am well and like my place very much. I have not been home sick yet. Frank – I ride up to Rocky Hill yesterday I saw Frank [Benjamin Francis] Mattoon and had a long talk with him he said that he wished that Milo had been in Hell more than a dozen times. I have not been up to Hartford yet but I am going up thare this week some time to get me some cloths. The names of the women are Miss Deilia Harris and Miss Martha Blinn and Miss Woolent they are all sisters, two of them has been married. Tell Gust that he must write again. I have got a chest of drawers to keep my things in. Give my love to Mother and Father and Charles and Charlotte and Annie and Lenny.

So good bye,

John E Mattoon

Tell Lenny that he must be a good boy and get all of Mothers' wood and I will bring him something nice when I come home.

John E Mattoon

It appears that John was luckier in his employers than Frank. The mysterious "Milo" must have been a terror. In a large household at home, John certainly had limited space for his personal items, and his wonder that "I have got a chest of drawers" speaks to the relative penury of his childhood. Whatever may have been the character of John's relationship with his parents, this postscript about his eight-year-old brother Leonard reveals that he was already the family-centered person he would remain in adulthood. His reluctance to tell too many stories that might cause pain to his family seemed always paired with a fierce interest in his family, and particularly in its younger members, Johns' siblings, nieces, and nephews.

June the 17th 1859
Wethersfield

Dear sister, [Sarah] I received your kind letter and was very glad to hear that you was well. I have not been home sick yet. I have got me a pair of pants that cost a dollar and a half and a linen coat that cost a dollar and a quarter and another pair of shoes that cost a dollar and nine pence that is twelve and a half cents. Charlotte wrote in her last letter that Bill had killed one of our pigs I should like to know which Bill it was. I ain't home sick only when I sing home sweet home in the night. The names of the women are Miss Delia Harris and Miss Martha and Miss Woocut I like my place very much give my love to mother and when you write father give my love to him give my love to George and Charley and Lot and Ann and Len but save a good portion of it for your self and C. H. [Charley Haight] Tell John Hen [Cousin John Henry Mattoon] that if he don't stop stealing that I will have to lick him tell him also that Frank [Mattoon] is so good too.

By John E Mattoon

I sleep with the man

The pants and linen coat indicate that John was paid reasonably well, and perhaps doubled as an indoor servant at times, in between planting and harvests perhaps, but there is no further evidence to confirm this. John would later refer in his letters to "Miss Delia" (Cordelia Harris) as "Aunt Delia" and asked to be remembered to her during the war. Religious allusions such as "I sleep with the man" were very rare in John's vernacular and virtually ceased as he grew older.

II.   Family

John E. Mattoon's father was William Smith Mattoon, who was born on February 5, 1807, the second of six children. He married Margaret Short on September 24, 1825 and died during John's military service on October 14, 1865. The family resided in the town of Canaan, New York in Columbia County, and eventually moved to the larger market town of Woodstock. J. H. French, in his *Gazetteer of New York* (1860), gave an excellent description of a vibrant community at the time:

> [Columbia] county was formed from Albany, April 4, 1786. It lies upon the e. bank of the Hudson, between Rensselaer and Dutchess cos., and extends e. to the Massachusetts line. It contains an area of 688 sq. mi., and is centrally distant 29 mi. from Albany. The Taghkanick Mts. extend along the e. border, and the adjoining parts of the co. are broken by numerous irregular ranges of hills which constitute the outlying spurs of those mountains. The w. part of the co. consists of an undulating plateau terminating in bluffs on the Hudson River. The principal streams are Roeliff Jansens Kill and Claverack and Kinderhook Creeks. Upon these streams and their tributaries are numerous valuable mill sites. The various branches of agriculture form the leading industrial pursuits of the people. Hay, (of which large quantities are pressed and sent to market,) rye, oats, corn, potatoes, and buckwheat, are the staple productions. Stock raising and dairying receive considerable attention. The manufacture of paper,

cotton fabrics, vegetable extracts, and iron, is largely carried on. A greater quantity of paper is made in this co. than in any other in the State, and the co. also takes precedence of all others in the amount of tinctures and extracts prepared from medicinal plants. The city of Hudson is the county seat. The courthouse and jail is a fine building, fronting on Washington Square. The poorhouse is a spacious brick building located upon a farm of 200 acres in Ghent. The most important works of internal improvement are the Hudson River R. R., extending through the w. part of the co., the Albany & West Stockbridge R. R., through the n. part, the Hudson & Boston R. R., terminating at Hudson, and the New York & Harlem R. R., terminating at Chatham Four corners. Four newspapers are published in the co.[7]

Canaan, New York is a lovely part of the world, with rivers, lakes, rolling hills and orchards. Captain Franklin Ellis, in his book *History of Columbia County, New York* (1878) described the hamlets of Canaan as a farming community not unlike any other during the war. "Canaan Four Corners a little east and north of the centre, is the largest village in the town, having a few hundred inhabitants. It is a station on the Boston and Albany railroad, and a point of considerable business. The location is in a pleasant valley, surrounded by high hills, which give it a secluded appearance. There are a Congregational church, several stores, and two hotels."[8] Canaan was in fact five communities: Canaan Four Corners, Queechy, Flat Brook, Canaan Center, Canaan, and Red Rock.

John was from a long line of New England farmers and soldiers. His grandfather Christopher was born in 1773, and fought in the war of 1812. His great-grandfather Gershom was born in Hebron, Connecticut in 1746. His great-great-grandfather (also Gershom), was born in Deerfield, Massachusetts in 1690. His great-great-great-grandfather was Philip Mattoon who was born in 1655 in either Ipswich, Massachusetts or Portland, New Hampshire, and became one of the original settlers of Deerfield, Massachusetts. Philip fought in King Philip's War, and was subsequently recruited by Captain William Turner for the defense of Western Massachusetts in 1676, participating in the Falls Fight in May of that year. Philip married Sarah Hawks of Hadley, Massachusetts in 1677. They were part of the original permanent settlement at Deerfield owning lot number 22 at least until 1714.[9] John's great-great-great-great-grandfather Hubartus Mattoon was born either in 1628 or 1630, and may have emigrated from England (probably via Holland) to New England some time prior to 1652. Hubartus was married on February 5, 1652 in Portsmouth, New Hampshire to Mary (or Margaret) Washington. He signed an oath of allegiance in Kittery, Maine to the Massachusetts Bay Company on November 16, 1652. There is also an alternative record for Hubartus indicating he was born in 1630 in Portsmouth, New Hampshire although this seems highly unlikely as Captain Walter Neal and his small following of Englishmen first sailed up the Piscataqua River in 1630. It is however reasonable to suggest that he emigrated earlier than 1652 and was a sworn member of the Portsmouth community in the early period, 1640 to 1650, when it was known as Strawbery Banke.[10]

John E. Mattoon was the seventh of nine children. The first was Harriet Elizabeth, born in 1831, who only lived to three years of age. The eldest living sibling, also a sister, was Mary Helen born in 1834, who married Milton Fitch. Then came Sarah Jane (1836) who married Charles (the other "Charley") Haight of New Lebanon, NY on November 20, 1857. John was very close to Charley Haight, worked for him before the war, and eventually married his sister. John's eldest brother, George Washington (1839) who in the common manner of eldest sons helped run the family farm, eventually bought his way out of the Union Army after running to Canada for a time. His next brother, Charles "Charley" Baldwin Mattoon (1841) went to war with the 5th Connecticut Infantry, Co. G; in July, 1861, later re-enlisted; and was discharged July 19, 1865. Charley eventually married Alice West and moved to Frederick, Maryland, where they raised seven children. The only letter in the collection addressed to John Mattoon is some brotherly advice on soldiering from Charley. The next sibling was another sister, Charlotte "Lot" Salisbury Mattoon (1843) who married Horace Crocker Bristol (whom John described as a "rich widower") on December 22, 1858. John himself was born in 1846, and then came a sister, Annie Elizabeth Mattoon (1848) who married Edward Huyck Stone II, and finally the baby of the family, Leonard "Lenny" Warner Mattoon, born in 1851. The siblings closest to John in birth order seem to be have been John's favorites as the majority of his Civil War letters are addressed to "Lot" or "Annie".

Existing evidence supports the assertion that the Mattoon family practiced the Methodist Episcopal religion. About a dozen Mattoon graves lie in the now abandoned Methodist graveyard west of Queechy Lake, New York including that of John's oldest brother George Washington Mattoon.[11] Captain Ellis in the History *of Columbia County* (1878) provides data that indicates the Mattoons likely worshipped at Trinity Methodist Episcopal Church at Red Rock in Canaan. "A plain but substantial meeting-house . . . is still used by the society. The church forms a part of the East Chatham circuit, and is served by pastors in that connection."[12] In the town at the time there were almost no Catholics, and the majority of parishioners were either Evangelical Lutheran, Methodist Episcopal, or Reformed.[13] Throughout the span of the *Mattoon Letters* John did not exhibit any predilection toward religion or religious thought. He was more than likely an "adherent" who, unlike a "member" was not publicly accountable for his Christian life and probably did not attend many church meetings at this Americanized offshoot of the Anglican Church. The Northern Methodist Episcopal Church split from the Southern Methodists in 1844 over the issue of slaveholding. Given the entire record it is unlikely that Church doctrine had any great influence on John Mattoon at all, despite the fact that America was in the midst of the Second Great Awakening. While religious revivalism had swept the nation it had less impact on the established Northern religions, with the Methodist Episcopal churches exhibiting the same aloof posture it had for generations.

Three cousins were very close to John in his childhood and later life, witnessed by the frequency with which his letters mention them. The first, John Henry "John Hen" Mattoon enlisted with John E. on the same day and fought in the *same Company*. "John Hen" (also of Canaan, NY) was the eldest son of John's uncle Benjamin Mattoon and Phebe Short (John E. Mattoon's mother's sister) and was one of 11 children. He was born on November 9, 1841 and was married to Jennie Foote in November of 1861. He was officially "discharged" from the Regiment on June 20, 1865 and died on June 10, 1915. Another close cousin was Thaddeus "Thad" H. Mattoon. Second son of Uncle Ben, Thad was born on June 29, 1843. He enlisted on August 6, 1862 in the NY 128th Regiment, Co. A, and was discharged July 12, 1865. He died on February 12, 1908. Last but not least was Frank Mattoon, (the third son of Uncle Ben) who was first mentioned when John was only fourteen, as living in Rocky Hill, Connecticut when John was in service in nearby Wethersfield. Later John would go absent without leave to visit Frank while his regiment was in Dismount Camp.[14] These two families made up of the Mattoon brothers marrying the Short sisters counted twenty four members between themselves.

III.   Back in Canaan, NY

Following the June 1859 letter there is a three-year gap in the epistolary record. Census records show John Mattoon residing in Wethersfield, Connecticut in the summer of 1860 and it is likely he worked for the sisters for at least two years. The next letter that has survived was written by John when he was back in Canaan, in the employ of his brother-in-law Charley Haight.

By the summer of 1863 John E. Mattoon knew all about the horrors of the war that by then had been raging for more than two years. His brother Charley (Charles Baldwin Mattoon, now aged twenty-two), serving with the 5th Connecticut, had fought in the bloody battle of Cedar Mountain, (an engagement of the 2nd Bull Run Campaign) on August 9, 1862. Shortly after this, on August 18, John told Charley (probably in response to a letter received describing Charley's experiences at Cedar Mountain), "I have got over my war fever and I guess it will stay for a little while."

John made mention of Charley having reported that only 16 members of his 60-man company made it out of Cedar Mountain unscathed. By then the sorry story of the battle was common knowledge: the Federal right had been soundly beaten and ran back through the Fifth's lines with the Confederates pursuing. The Fifth sustained over fifty percent casualties because they chose to stand and fight.[15] Like many men sitting on the sidelines, John was conflicted about the War. In the same letter John showed a mix of nascent patriotism and an attempt to assuage his brother's shame at the Army's total defeat: "you must write to me and tell me all of the particular . . . you have had your turn at skeddaddling by and by you will give them dam rebels Hell, I hope you will anyway." He also noted the names of the men from Canaan who had already left for war, including their cousin Thaddeus Mattoon who enlisted August 6, 1862 in the 128th New York Infantry.[16]

In a letter to Charley Mattoon dated October, 1862, John talked of enlisting as well. Then in April of 1863 he noted that eldest brother George had "sold his cow and his pig and his hens" and was off to "Canaday" to avoid the coming draft leaving a new-born son behind. Distain clearly showing through, John announced: "I don't believe I shall run from the draft by God."[17] It is entirely possible that his unrelenting hardness of character in the face of future events was forged in his negative relationship with his father and eldest brother, both of whom he rarely mentioned in his letters, other than to criticize them. John Mattoon, through his actions, surely wanted to prove his worth, both to them and to himself. His future decisions likely were partially influenced by these relationships. However at this time in his life, John was still battling his "war fever". This fever was primarily a lust for adventure mixed with a secondary need for public and family affirmation. A distant third was a still forming sense of duty. In all of the early letters there is not one indication that two of the biggest moral ideologies of the period, religion and slavery (pro or con) had any bearing on his future decisions.

More news was sent to Charley from John in a letter in July, 1863. A mutual friend, Nelson Ellsworth, had returned home from the War with some "pretty hard stories." According to the New York State Archives, Nelson was from nearby Austerlitz, New York, and was twenty-one when he first saw service in the New York First Mounted Rifles. On January 4, 1864 he re-enlisted with the 4th New York Provincial Cavalry. He was finally mustered out on November 29, 1865. And again, in August of 1863 John wrote Charley Mattoon while sitting across from his brother in law and employer, Charley Haight.

[No date – est. August, 1863]

Brother Charley,

I received your letter to night and a ticklier cuss you never see. I tell you, you told me to take your advice and not inlist. Well Charley I guess I will my war fever is all off now and I hope it will stay off a little while don't you? Our folks are all well now. I included thare is no new news to write now only that Rushe Johnson had got another job so haight is writing on the other side of the table and his pen is making such a hell of a scratching that I can't think of much to write but I will do the best I can and that won't be any to good. Thad Mattoon has inlisted and is now in Hudson a drilling he says he likes it first rate so far. The darn young one is a squalling so I can't write worth a shit. Well Charley we have not got through haying yet and I guess we never shall. I hope not anyway. You said you had had a big fight I am dam glad you did not get hit. Tell bill Fields to write to me tell him all of Parsons his folks are well ther is that darn child of Charleys a squalking! By God I guess I shall go crazy. Cuss the flies how they do bite. I swear I can't write thare. That darn young one has struck up again, here it is 10 o'clock and I have 3 more letters to write, by gosh Charley I can't write much more. Charley I want you to write to me oftener that you have done for there is nothing I like Better that to go down to the Post office and look in Box number 46 and see a letter in thare for me. I can't write any more this time so I will bid you good night and pleasant dreams, I hope you will have.

J E mattoon

It appears that John, now a restless 17-year-old, was annoyed and worn down by his life of labor on a working farm. He expressed his exasperation over farm routines with an adolescent's cynicism: "Well Charley, we have not got through haying yet and I guess we never shall, I hope not anyway."

The newspapers had been full of reports of the thrashings the Confederate Army had been inflicting on the Union Army for two years. The daunting mortality rate in battle as well as that from disease was starting to become better known publicly. In the face of these facts, what would lead a young farmer to volunteer to join the carnage? It seems that despite growing public awareness of the war's gruesome costs and public impatience with incompetent Union commanders, public morale fueled by a fierce patriotism still ran high through most of the North. With most of his friends and many family members already wearing Union blue, John didn't "get over [his] war fever" for good.

There is an added dimension of community and political orientation in John's dilatory attitude toward the War. It appears that his family and much of his community were Democrats. It is important however, to note that they were not considered "Copperheads" but "War Democrats"[18] who were a more conservative part of the now splintered Democratic Party. At the grass-roots level Copperheads or "Peace Democrats" were mostly Midwesterners who asserted that the Republicans had provoked the South into secession. They claimed that the War was designed to limit states rights and create racial equality, both anathema, and most importantly (in the period 1861–1863) that military means had failed and would never restore the Union. They were branded as traitors or at best defeatists and Southern sympathizers by Republicans. War Democrats, or "Union" Democrats, were conservative-leaning and did not object to the war, just to the policies of Lincoln and the Republican Congress. They could be called at times agrarian and nativist, but they did not admire the Southern way of life. For them, the object of the war was the preservation of the Union and generally *not* the abolition of slavery.

Political orientation and the events of the 1864 election with their effect on the common soldier will be discussed in more detail, but it is useful to note that "Emancipation as an aim of the war was simply not an issue for New York State farmers."[19] In fact, during the 1860 elections in Columbia County, New York, Abraham Lincoln won by only 5108 to 4722 votes. The county also voted on "popular questions", one of which was "For equal suffrage for colored persons." It was voted down by a vote of 5646 to 1881.[20] Even though a "War" Democrat, there can be no doubt that John's political orientation created at least some additional impediments to any decision to enlist.

IV.   Recruiting the Second Wave

The 21st New York Cavalry was gathered from Rochester and Troy, New York and their surrounding communities. It had as its nucleus many veterans of the 2nd New York Infantry under then Major William Badger Tibbits, who had first been commissioned in May of 1861. After a number of bloody engagements, of the original eleven hundred men in that command, only three hundred eighty six returned to Troy in May of 1863.[21]

Col. Tibbits was a lawyer and manufacturer and the scion of a family of successful businessmen in upper New York State. Their political connections were sufficiently weighty to compel New York's Democratic Governor, Horatio Seymour to find Tibbits a command of his own. While awaiting the opportunity to raise a regiment, another veteran, Major Charles Fitz Simmons of the Rochester, New York based Black Horse Cavalry (formed of the City's Volunteer Dragoons) was also at loose ends.   The two men were soon put together by the War Department, with Tibbits as Colonel, and Fitz Simmons at Lt. Colonel of a new cavalry regiment.[22] Their sponsor would be New York Congressman John A. Griswold, who immediately pledged $1,000 toward a bounty fund for the "Griswold Light Cavalry". The Tibbits family was Democratic and "related by blood and affinity to Martin Van Buren" (1782-1862) the eighth President of the U. S. and a powerful political force from nearby Kinderhook, New York.[23] Col. Tibbits' political reputation may have attracted to the regiment a larger than expected group of young Democrats from the surrounding region.

Recruiting in the middle year of the Civil War was haphazard and cutthroat. Tibbits advertised in the *Troy* [NY] *Times* for recruits, offering re-enlisters $522 and new recruits $166. These were huge sums, and indicative of the increasing difficulty of recruiting volunteer regiments. The Troy City Council also offered $50 for veterans and $72 for recruits.[24] At the same time, Fitz Simmons was setting up recruiting in his part of the state.

The Civil War marked the first time (on either side) that soldiers were drafted into service. In March of 1863, the National Conscription Act was passed by the Union. Draftees would now be called by lottery. The Confederate States had a draft law in effect since April of 1862. Once called, a draftee had the opportunity to either pay a commutation fee of $300 to be exempt from the draft, or to hire a replacement that would exempt him from the entire war. By

·

June of 1863, Rensselaer County, New York, announced a Federal draft quota of 1,800 men from which volunteer recruits could be credited against.[25] Any men that could be pulled into units through the use of bounties would offset the numbers needed by the draft. Charges of class discrimination were leveled against the draft laws since exemption and commutation clauses and other loopholes they allowed propertied men to avoid service, unfairly targeting the immigrant and poor populations. This sweeping new law enacted by both the North and South, was poorly prosecuted and unwieldy as well as being immensely unpopular. Many conscripts simply failed to report for duty. "Under the Union draft act men faced the possibility of conscription in July 1863 and in Mar., July, and Dec. 1864. Of the 249,259 eighteen-to-thirty five-year-old men whose names were drawn, only about six percent served, the rest paying commutation or hiring a substitute."[26]

The New York Draft Riots of July 13-17, 1863 were a constant reminder that the ardent patriots, abolitionists, hotheads and zealots were already dressed in Union Blue. A conscription system that allowed wealthier citizens to buy out of the war incensed tens of thousands of mostly Irish Catholics, who rioted for four days in what many historians consider the worst civil unrest in American history.

All of the surrounding villages had to contribute to the draft quota by recruiting local youth. Even before the draft, Canaan recognized the need to recruit: "A special meeting was held August 30, 1862, to facilitate enlistments, a bounty of $150 per volunteer being provided to this end. The supervisor and the assessors constituted a disbursing committee of the several bounty funds provided at this and subsequent special meetings. The soldier's list gives the names of the volunteers credited to the town [of Canaan] by the State authorities."[27] By the time the draft was instituted in 1863, up to $325 could have been earned by Columbia County enlistees. The little villages of Canaan provided one hundred fifty five men in total for the war effort and $65,452 was paid in bounties (of which only $22,500 was reimbursed by the state, a crushing debt for the small town) and eleven men including eldest brother George Washington Mattoon provided substitutes to fight for them.[28]

Rural American men's decisions about joining the Army were inevitably affected by the changing economics and culture of agriculture. As farming increasingly became a cost-intensive business dependent on unpredictable markets rather than a self-sufficient way of life, many individuals drifted away from it, often because they could not afford to buy enough land to make farming pay. "By 1860, an eighty-acre farm in Illinois required nearly $1700 in initial outlays. Increasingly prospective farmers began their careers as tenants, hoping to save enough money to purchase their own farm. These farm laborers often formed the core of volunteers. Many saw a soldier's enlistment bounties as a gift-wrapped down payment for acreage."[29] The story was very similar in New York State. Capital was necessary as a preliminary goal even as the use of credit facilities was gradually expanding. There is no question that John Mattoon yearned for the "yeoman ideal of the independent self-sufficient freeman who operated his own family-sized farm."[30] But John was not even at the tenancy stage. What better way to earn money, have some adventures and see the world?

One of the vagaries of the recruiting process in the Civil War was that the initial companies of a regiment could be sent off while recruiting continued. Following this pattern the Griswold Light Cavalry were mustered in as follows: A, B, C and D on August 28, 1863; E on September 1, 1863; F on September 18, 1863; G October 14, 1863; H on October 15, 1863; I on October 16, 1863; K on November; and L and M in January, 1864. Companies A through E left New York State for Washington, D.C. on September 4, 1863. Company F left on September 19; G to I on October 19; and K in November of 1863.[31] The last two Companies were proving hard to form, and to squeeze the last men out of the surrounding towns, unusually large bounties were instituted. In December, men who enlisted in the Regiment also drew a supplementary bounty of $300 if they were from Monroe County, NY.[32] Those Companies L and M did not leave until February of 1864.

Notes

1.   This quote is from a book review that historian Bruce Catton wrote on Bell Wiley's *Life of Billy Yank* (1951) in which Catton recognized the continuing need for a social history of the common soldier in the Civil War. Wiley was the first to write on the average soldier with *Life of Johnny Reb* (1943). "Review of Life of Johnny Reb", *Journal of Southern History* (Vol. 18, No. 4, Nov. 1952), 516-17

2.   Census records indicate that the Blinn family numbered dozens in Canaan, New York. Canaan was one of 19 towns that encompassed Columbia County in the middle-eastern portion of the state near the convergence of the Massachusetts and Connecticut borders. The hamlets that made up Canaan had a population of 2,193 in 1860. Capt. Franklin Ellis. *History of Columbia County, New York.* (New York: 1878), 136

3.   Ibid., 359

4.   *United States Federal Census, Town of Wethersfield, Hartford County, State of Connecticut.* (25 June 1860), 28; (20 July 1870), 42

5.   John E. Mattoon to Annie Mattoon Stone. *John E. Mattoon Letters*, Collection of the Author (March 17, 1865)

6.   John E. Mattoon to Annie Mattoon Stone *Mattoon Letters*, (December 18, 1865)

7.   J. H. French, *Gazetteer of New York*, (Syracuse, NY: R.P. Smith Co. 1860) 241

8.   Ellis, 325

9.   Lillian G. Mattoon and Donald P. Mattoon, (eds.) *Genealogy of the Descendants of Philip Mattoon, of Deerfield Massachusetts.* (Littleton, NH:

Courier Printing Co. 1965) Generational references: 1-5, 11, 23, 47, 86, 138-39, A-30

10.   The Church of Jesus Christ of Latter-day Saints, *Ancestral File #: N8BD-PJ (R)* (Repository: Family History Library, Salt Lake City, UT: June 1998, data as of 5 January 1998)

11.   Rickard, Lawrence. *Columbia County Master Cemetery List.* Columbia County Historical Society, Kinderhook, NY. The graveyard can be found at Lat: 42°24' 06" N; Lon: 73°25' 19" W.

12.   Ellis, 356

13.   Ibid., 126

14.   See footnote 4 for similarly marked citations in Mattoon, also John E. Mattoon to Horace Bristol, *Mattoon Letters*, (August, 27, 1864)

15.   Mark M. Boatner. *The Civil War Dictionary.* (New York: David McKay Co. Inc. 1959), 134

16.   Ellis, 421-22

17.   John E. Mattoon to Charles Mattoon, *Mattoon Papers*, (April 22, 1863)

18.   See Joanna Cowden, "The Politics of Dissent: Civil War Democrats in Connecticut." *New England Quarterly*, (Vol.56, No.4, Dec. 1983) for a good discussion of the views of Northeastern Democrats.

19.   T. Harry Williams. "Citizen Soldiers of the Civil War". *Mississippi Valley Historical Review*, (Vol. 31, No. 2, Sep. 1944), 191

20.   Ellis, 48-52

21.   Reed, 17-18

22.   Ibid., 23

23.   Ibid., 4

24.   *Troy Daily Times*, (Troy, NY., July 25, 1863, 3 col. 4)

25.   Reed, 35

26.   Patricia L. Faust (ed.). *Historical Times Encyclopedia of the Civil War.* (NY: Harper & Row. 1986), 112

27.   Ibid., 372-3

28.   Ibid., 150

29.   Drew E. VandeCreek, *Economic Development and Labor in Civil War Illinois*, in: http://dig.lib.niu.edu/civilwar/economic.html (2002) 2, Accessed 3/12/06

30.   Clarence H. Danhof. Farm-making Costs and the Safety Valve: 1850-1860. *Journal of Political Economy*, (Vol. 69, No. 3, June 1941), 349

31.   Reed, 35-54

32.   *The Rochester Union & Advertiser*, Rochester, NY., (November 14, 1863, 1 Col. 2)

CHAPTER TWO

I.   Why Fight?

As this story is as much about why John Mattoon chose to fight as it is about his perseverance it is important to review and keep in mind modern Civil War historiography on the common soldier's motivation. There is a multitude of work that has been published in the past but certain historians come to mind when discussing the common soldier of the Civil War. Gerald Linderman who wrote *Embattled Courage* (1987) is known for his study of early Union enlistees who he categorized as progressively disillusioned with the political ideals of the War. This thesis does not really apply to John Mattoon, who enlisted later and unlike the men that rushed off to war right after the news of Fort Sumter, exhibited virtually no political or moral ideals before his service began. Many aspects of James McPherson's *For Cause and Comrades* (1997) in which the author states that initial political motivation remained a critical motivating component for soldiers throughout the War also does not fit at all with the elements of John's early motivations. Finally, there were certainly no romantic connotations floating through John's head as the horror of war was by now well known to all.

Yet late in 1863 John E. Mattoon made the decision to go to war. It patently was not a decision based on political, moral or patriotic views. Adventure away from home and the aforementioned need for community and particularly family approbation, along with a nascent component of "duty" provided the individual impetus. The specter of the draft hanging over his head and the positive economic considerations finally must have been compelling enough to push John forward.

John's brother Charley Mattoon had enlisted first, and then his cousins Thaddeus Mattoon, (August 6, 1862) and Benjamin F. Mattoon (October 31, 1862). Their friend Orlando Wariner of Canaan enlisted in Company A of the 21st New York Cavalry on December 29, 1863, and it was surely from his experience that John found out about the Regiment and eventually made his way to the 21st Cavalry recruiting center in Troy, New York and from there to Elmira, where initial encampment, mustering-in and drilling occurred.

One thing John had evidently fixated upon was the commonly held belief that cavalry duty was safer than infantry duty and much more glamorous. It was widely thought that "cavalry scouted, established outposts and mounted pickets. Mounted units rode to work and suffered few casualties."[1] Something else that was likely on a potential enlistee's mind in the summer of 1863 was that the tide of war was finally turning against the South. Gen. Robert E. Lee's seemingly invincible Army of Northern Virginia had finally been soundly defeated at the momentous Battle of Gettysburg (July 1–3) in Pennsylvania. John had no way of knowing that the character of the war was soon to change in ways that made it more hazardous for cavalrymen, as an increasingly desperate enemy turned more and more to the tactics of Confederate Col. John S. Mosby's guerillas which he would see first-hand in the Shenandoah Valley.

Both John E. and John H. Mattoon enlisted in Company L on January 4, 1864, and were mustered in a day later. Some of the fear of the unknown was mitigated by the two cousins having the company of a few other Canaan area boys at the same time. Being mustered in apparently did not mean joining the regiment as John drafted a rather cryptic note to Charley Haight on January 20, 1864: "I am here in Canaan now, but I have got to go to Poughkeepsie this afternoon, so I will send Len [youngest brother Leonard Mattoon was now 13] up there. I want you to send me 10 dollars by Len in an envelope. The provost marshal sent me after the other boys. We have got to go to Almyra [Elmira, New York] on Friday next so you will not see me again." Eventually, Companies L and M shipped out in February, the last enlistees of the 21st New York Cavalry to be sent for training.

Fred Shannon, in his useful book *The Organization and Administration of the Union Army 1861–1865* (1928) put a monetary cost to the increasing disinterest amongst young men in enlistment. He stated that by the end of the war, the Federal government had paid over $300,000,000 in bounties, and the Union states along with local agencies matched that number. Total bounty payments for the war were approximately $750,000,000. The bounties were quite large sums of money in the 1860s and encouraged all manner of corruption though such practices as "bounty jumping" whereby men would enlist in multiple companies and desert over and over again. However they were an effective tool for recruitment, and there is a strong indication that for John Mattoon the "greenbacks" were the final enticement. The "Canaan boy" knew that the reason for joining regiments recruited in the larger cities was simply that the wealthier districts gave larger bounties.

John wrote to Annie from the war front in July of 1864 "I got my state bounty the other day it is in the form of a $50 cheque."[2] That the money was still coming in during their service indicates a commitment to retaining what was left of the enlistees, at least for a while. What the Union cavalry could not have known was that this conflicted young farmer would end up showing a toughness and single-minded dedication to duty that was sadly lacking in many of his comrades. What John could not have known were the eventual consequences his vacillations were to cause when he became one of the last three-year cavalrymen mustered into his volunteer regiment that February of 1864.

II.   In the Army

"The Empire State furnished the most men and sustained the heaviest loss of any State in the War. It sent 448,850 men to the Union Armies, of whom 19,085 were killed in battle, while 27,449 more lost their lives from other causes while in the service; a total of 46,534 deaths."[3]

1,752 officers and men (including replacements) served in the 21st New York Cavalry Regiment from June 1863 to September 1866. The two cities where the most recruiting was done, Rochester and Troy, New York, being manufacturing towns were less homogeneous than might be expected with rather large ethnic populations for the time. A review of the Regimental Roll indicates approximately seventy percent of English heritage, fifteen percent Irish, five percent German, and a mix of Welsh, French, and Scottish for the rest. "The majority of the men enlisted in Troy were either farmers or laborers."[4] The laborers were mostly urban and had very little experience with horses. Many could not ride at all. The farmers may have understood horses quite well, but few rode them in the course of their work.

William Fox published a fascinating book entitled *Regimental Losses in the American Civil War 1861-1865* in 1889. It compiles a wealth of statistics from official records. His work provides a valuable if not terribly scientific basis for analyzing comparatively the demographic composition of the 21st New York Cavalry. According to Fox, the mean age of all the soldiers in the war was twenty five years. When classed by ages, the largest class was eighteen years of age, or 133,475 men. Out of 2,000,000 men, three-fourths were native-born Americans. Of the rest, Germany furnished 175,000; Ireland, 150,000; England, 50,000; British America, 50,000; other countries, 75,000.

Fox reported that the average height of Union troops was 5 feet 8 1/4 inches, and the average weight was 143 1/2 pounds. Forty eight percent were farmers; twenty four percent mechanics; sixteen percent laborers; five percent engaged in commercial pursuits; three percent were professional men; and four percent declared miscellaneous vocations.[5] Judging from these figures it appears that John E. Mattoon was around the size and certainly of the same class as the average Union private. He described himself as about ten pounds lighter than that average initially, but soon was "getting fat fast" on Army food. John's service record described him as "Born in Canaan, NY. Occupation farmer. Blue eyes, dark-hair, light complexion. Height 5ft. 9 ½ in."[6]

The men of the Griswold Lights were almost all long-term (three-year) enlistees. When the initial allure of patriotic military service wore off and the enormity of what they had bargained for hit home a number of them started to desert. Some desertions can be put down to bounty jumping, but one biographer of the 21st NY Cavalry reported the actual number was small "with the total number of bounty-jumpers probably no more than 75 men."[7] Thomas Reed's review of the *Adjutant General's Record*, State of New York (1868) indicates that 104 men, or over eight percent of the initial roster of approximately one thousand two hundred, deserted within the first sixty days after mustering in.[8] A review of the Regimental Roster indicates that each of the companies as they reported in had about seven men desert en route to their assigned dismounted training at Staten Island, New York nearby Manhattan for dismounted training.[9]

The first elements of the 21st New York arrived on Staten Island, New York in September of 1863. In their camp at New Dorp they were to receive a course of basic military training. The routine included marching in time without arms while moving in columns of companies. After a few days of this the recruits were supposed to move on to an intensive two months of cavalry training on horses learning cavalry tactics near the nation's capital.[10] New Dorp was the site of initial attempts to make volunteer cavalrymen into soldiers, but apparently that process was not always accomplished successfully. Richard Arthur, who served in Company A of the 21st New York, was on Staten Island in September of 1863. He described a riot in camp that resulted in four deaths from gunshots and the throwing of rocks. Unfortunately he did not detail the reason for the riot.[11] John Mattoon's Company L did not arrive at Staten Island until long afterward, in February of 1864. With barely enough time to learn what "Boots and Saddles" meant (the famous bugle call that is the signal for mounted drill and the un-official anthem of the cavalry), John was shipped out again only two weeks later.

Mattoon sent his most interesting letters to his brothers or other male relatives. They add more gritty details and expressions of exuberance that do not appear in the letters he wrote for his sisters, in which he knew he had to be more circumspect. Letters Mattoon sent to a brother-in-law and a brother comment colorfully on his trip to mounted training camp. Companies L and M of the 21st New York had been packed onto a steamer converted into a large troop ship for the trip of two to three days to Annapolis, MD. Then they went by rail north to Washington, DC and finally arrived at Camp Stoneman, a part of the immense cavalry depot system based at Giesboro, District of Columbia under the Chief of Cavalry, General George Stoneman. For whatever reason, they were carefully guarded, perhaps against desertion. The trip was certainly memorable:

Alexandria, [VA] Sunday Feb. 21st 1864

Brother Horace [Charlotte's husband, Horace Bristol]

How are you?

Here I be down in Alexandria and am like to stay here for three or four years. It is the darndest hole you have ever seen. We are all fixed up in a room about 2 inches one way and 3 the other but we have bully fodder: it consists of one slice of pork, 1 slice of bread and all the coffee we want. So we live pretty fast. I tell you we had the darndest time a-getting here. They drove us on board of an old transport and piled us in about 40 deep. We had to sleep upon the upper deck but darn little did we sleep. When we had been about 2 days the boys began to get sea sick and such spewing you never see. I am well now and won't be sick rite away I don't believe. The boys have got the musills here and a speckelded lot of boys have drunk rum (puts me in a mind I would like a little) but no use of talking for I can't get any, so I am going to get along with out it. That's what the matter is, I wish I had your old [hard] cider barrel down here about half an hour or so. I don't think you would have much vinegar to sell another year but it is some consolation to know that when I get home I can wade in it. Ha ha! Only about 34 months [left to serve]. I can't think of much to write only that the boys from Canaan are all well. I bought me a pair of [cavalry] boots the other day and paid 10 dollars for them. The lugs come up to my knees and about 40 feet farther. Give my respects to all the girls you happen to come across and tell them that I ain't dead that's all. Tell Lot that she must take good care of her self. I can't think of any thing new more now so I will just dry up. Yours,

John E Mattoon
Alias
Snay

Bully Ike

Ten dollars was a great deal of money and "Snay" must have been proud of his new knee-high cavalry boots, which were not standard issue by any means. Drinking when at all practicable was a much sought-after pastime perhaps only equaled by chewing tobacco or pipe smoking for the common soldier. John often mentioned the "cider barrel" at home and was referring to apple cider kept after the fall pressing in Canaan for the express purpose of fermentation as an alcoholic beverage.

John wrote a week later to his brother Charles Mattoon on active duty with the 5th Connecticut. He was excited to see the world and felt raring to go:

Camp Stoneman
Feb 28th, 1864

Brother Charley,

We left Alexandria on the 24th and came to Washington. Then we marched up here to camp and here we have been since. We have bully times here I tell you we have a place about 4 miles square to run around in. It seems like home here, it seems as though we had bust out of prison. We was shut up in Alexandria for a week and never went out of doors while I was there without a guard. I don't know how long we will stay here but I guess not a great while. The boys are all well and feeling first rate. [George] Smoke Barnes says he wishes he was back in old Canaan but I have not seen enough of soldiering yet. John Hen [ry Mattoon] is growing as poor as an old crow but I grow fat. I tell you I weighed myself the other day and guess how much I weigh. I weighed when I left Poughipsie [Pougkeepsie, New York] just 132 lbs. and now I weigh 148 if that ain't getting fat fast then I don't know what is. We have not got our arms or horses yet. There is about a thousand dismounted cavalry here [and] we have all the fresh beef we want to eat. Vic, Smoke Barnes, George Smith[12] and I all tent together. We have to sleep on the ground with nothing under us but our blankets. I can't write any more now for I have got to go and drill.

John E. Mattoon

By the time John Mattoon got to the cavalry depot at Geisboro Point the installation was still only about seven months old. It was originally built to accommodate up to 12,000 horses and included "a mess-house, tent quarters, quartermaster supplies, a chapel, and training facilities."[13] Geisboro and its surrounding camps (particularly Camp Stoneman) were also "remount" facilities for elements of units in the field who had lost horses to conflict or disease, and served as logistical support depots for all Federal cavalry units in the eastern theater of operations. The whole system was the successful product of Congressional legislation that created the Cavalry Bureau in July of 1863 in direct response to the early successes of the Confederate cavalry in the War. There were six depots in all, and they made a large impact on the prosecution of the war after late 1863, specifically addressing earlier problems the Union faced training and supplying new cavalry.[14]

Each of the new troopers of the 21st New York Cavalry received a horse and a uniform consisting of only a short, close fitting blouse, or "shell", cavalry trousers and a slouch or "forage" hat. Additionally each trooper received an unsharpened Model 1860 saber, (shorter and lighter than the old "wrist breaker" 1840 pattern) two revolvers in saddle holsters, a Burnside's Carbine and a McClellan saddle.[15] The Burnside single shot breech loading carbine was designed in the 1850's by Union Gen. Ambrose Burnside of the Burnside Rifle Co. of Providence, Rhode Island. It fired a .54 caliber ball set in a tube of wax paper (later drawn brass) which held the charge. This rifle-barreled carbine was a finely made and well balanced weapon of seven pounds in weight with a total length of 39 ½ inches. It was used primarily by volunteer cavalry units. The government eventually procured more than 55,000 of them along with 22,000,000 cartridges.[16] The revolvers could have been .36 or .44 Colts, Remingtons, or even Whitneys or Starrs. Records do not indicate which model the troopers received.[17] They were all percussion revolvers that needed each cylinder to be individually charged with powder and ball and then topped with a percussion cap at the rear. While mechanically quite modern, most patterns were subject to sympathetic detonation of all cylinders at once, and performed poorly given any form of wetness in the field.

From the start of the war until the mid-point in 1863 the Confederate cavalry was convincingly better in the field than their Union counterpart. There was a real difference between young men of the North and the South. Although perhaps too much of a generalization, Southern men were out of doors more than men up north where industrialization spurred rapid growth of cities and commercial or indoor pastimes were more plentiful. Southerners were actively engaged in a country life which included equestrian pursuits. Horses were an integral part of life in all of America, but were more intertwined into the social fabric in the South. Both hunting and horseracing were hugely popular sports for instance. In the case of Southern cavalry, recruitment included bringing your own horse with you and de facto precluded the need for much basic training. The Confederate government then paid the trooper a stipend for feed and care. This had the initial effect of creating high quality cavalry regiments. Yet Southern cavalrymen only received compensation if their horse was killed in battle, not by injury, disease or malnutrition. What followed was a general lack of horses as the war progressed, and combined with substantially less ability to provide arms and accouterments eventually led to the eclipse of the Confederate Cavalry.

For the Union it was not material that was needed nor was there a lack of motivated men. What was missing was competent training and leadership. For John Mattoon and the "boys from Canaan" Union cavalry training was much improved by late 1863 and the men of the 21st New York Cavalry saw it first hand as their training became steadily more intense. The troopers had to learn the intricacies (and drudgery) of horse care and riding, along with saber and cavalry drill and basic un-mounted and mounted cavalry tactics.

The rudiments of learning to ride presented the largest problem. Even the young farmers of the regiment were not generally used to riding horses for any length of time. Draft animals were ridden occasionally, but almost always bareback, so that most troopers found the U.S. Army 1859 bit and bridle alien, and the McClellan saddle with its high front "Western" pommel highly uncomfortable.[18] The additional weight of a seven pound carbine on a sling, a saber, revolver, ammunition, and miscellaneous trappings made the training only more difficult and demanding. U.S. Army regulations called for more than fifty pounds of equipment in saddle bags.[19] As the troopers became more proficient, the training at last was taken into the field and the 21st performed some practice reconnaissance missions or "scouts" in non-combatant areas of Maryland. Several days were spent in the field and evaluations of cavalry tactics, horse care, and other skills proved positive.[20]

The role of the Civil War sutler was important. Outfitting and provisioning was terribly important in the Civil War. Sutlers were the purveyors of nonmilitary supplies to the regiment, such as tobacco, coffee and sugar. The articles of war stated that "persons permitted to sutle shall supply the soldiers with good and wholesome provisions or other articles at a reasonable price."[21] Unfortunately as a practical matter this was rarely the case. If they were on-post, sutlers had to be licensed by the commanding officer. Off-post, no rules applied and most anything could be bought if the price could be paid. While sutlers provided what the government would not for a cost, regimental quartermasters were supposed to provide the basics. Although most did their best to provide for the men, there were a multitude of scandals regarding the poor quality of provisions produced by unscrupulous parties and bought with the collusion of quartermasters for their troops.

The Regiment was formed into twelve companies, or troops, of eighty to one hundred men or ideally at full complement twelve hundred men. Each company was commanded by a captain under which served a first and second lieutenant, non-commissioned officers, and other staff. Companies were generally grouped into three battalions composed of four companies, each battalion commanded by a major. As the war ground on, these company numbers proved unsustainable due to desertion, disease, actual battle casualties and a general lack of horses. Most historians agree that at any given time the *average* Union cavalry regiment in the Civil War could muster for service barely half its official complement of troopers or around five hundred men. John Bonnell, after reviewing the muster rolls concluded: "The companies of the 21st New York averaged about eighty men when mustered into Federal service, but by the summer of 1864, sometimes less than half these numbers were available for service."[22] By October of 1864 John Mattoon reported to his sister Annie: "our Company has got enough to tend to right now, there was about 75 Rebs seen yesterday about 5 miles from here and there is only about 40 of us all told."[23]

The 21st New York was sent into in the field in January of 1864. A rear echelon remained at Camp Stoneman to train companies L and M which had not left New York yet. The regiment was ordered to Harper's Ferry and then to ride through Rebel held territory to Charlestown, West Virginia. Upon arrival on January 14, the 21st acted on standing orders to help the Army of the Potomac in the move up the Shenandoah Valley by providing anti-guerilla and security missions.[24] The long supply trains which originated at Harper's Ferry and needed to run the gauntlet through the Shenandoah Valley had to be protected from Confederate forces that ranged from partisan rangers roving in small bands all the way up larger commands such as Col. John S. Mosby's 43rd Virginia Cavalry.

In an attempt to create a strong fighting force, the 21st was combined (for operational purposes only) with the veteran 1st New York (Lincoln) Cavalry, which was in the process of re-enlistment woes after having been in the field for two years. Bad feelings existed between "veteran" units and the newer regiments built upon enlistment bounties. Veterans who saw themselves as tested soldiers and patriotic adventurers looked down on green newcomers they regarded as money-grubbing mercenaries, and there was at least one serious instance of shots fired between the two camps in January.[25] The *Troy* (NY) *Daily Times* of January 25, 1864 contains their correspondent's report:

> Well, the Twenty-first have been under fire for the first time, though I am sorry to say it was not against the enemies of the Union. Yesterday afternoon, some fifty or sixty men from the First New York cavalry, who were encamped near us, and who were evidently under the influence of lager beer, made a raid on our camp, and cut loose some men who were tied up by the wrist to trees, undergoing punishment for misdemeanor committed on the march to this place. They stated very boisterously that they did not allow any of their officers to inflict any kind of punishment upon them, and would not allow any men near them to be punished previous to a court-martial. Our officers and men were busily engaged in arranging our camp, and were entirely unprepared for any such proceedings, as we had no guard on at the time. A guard was immediately put around the camp, the men who were cut loose were again secured, and everything was quiet along our lines. Later in the day, some sixty men, braced up with more lager and armed with revolvers, made another rally upon our guard tent. The guard were drawn up in line, and being reinforced by a number of our officers, armed with carbines and revolvers, made a stand against the insurrectionists. Some sixty or seventy shots were exchanged, when the rioters were driven back to their own camp. News of the transaction was conveyed to the Ninety-eighth regiment, Pennsylvania infantry, who were stationed at Charlestown, some half-a-mile distant, and who marched immediately to the scene of insurrection. Some sixteen of the ringleaders were arrested and lodged in jail at Harper's Ferry, and as they can be identified by a number of our officers and men, they will no doubt be severely punished as they richly merit. Our casualties are one private, of Co. K., wounded in the leg, and two horses killed. Loss of the rioters: one wounded and sixteen taken prisoners. Everything is now tranquil. I must state in justification of the officers of the First New York cavalry, that they done everything in their power to quell the disturbance and aid in suppressing the riot. [26]

The winter of 1864 was cruelly cold in the Shenandoah Valley. As a result, skirmishes and pitched fights were rare. The Griswold Light Cavalry lost its first men to enemy fire in an extended five-day raid on Moorfield, West Virginia ending on the Fifth of February. They continued picket duty and guarded a variety of installations and wagon trains.

One of the most important functions of cavalry in the Civil War was as pickets. Picket duty was for the protection of the entire army, and whole regiments were assigned to this duty alone. It involved creating a ring or "picket line" around the camp to guard from attack, as well as scouting out the enemy and alerting the main body of danger. Long-range pickets could be over two miles away or farther, while the second guard and reserves held at the perimeter of the camp.

Col. Tibbits had elected to stay behind and supervise the training of the remaining two companies L and M at Giesboro. On March 8, 1864 Tibbits (with John Mattoon for the first time on operational duty in Company L) set out for Halltown, West Virginia with the two new companies and accepted command on March 9th, bringing the regiment to full strength.[27]

The only letter in the Mattoon collection posted to John was dated in late March and came from his older brother Charles "Charley" Baldwin Mattoon. There are very clear indications that much of John Mattoon's initial indecision and immaturity receded rapidly as he gained a better understanding of the reality of soldiering through his brother. He was also fully aware of Charlie's heroic sacrifices since his enlistment in July of 1861. John was devoted to Charley and certainly looked up to him as a role model. In the letter he received some valuable schooling about shooting his mouth off regarding his health, which amazingly remained strong throughout his service. (Though John did suggest in a lost letter to Charley that he desired some sought after down-time in a warm, dry hospital, perhaps for one of the less invasive diseases like dysentery). Most importantly Charley gave John guidance on what duty to his Country really meant in just six words: "I am rite to serve here".

Dechard Station, Tenn
March 26th 1864

Dear Brother,

I received your letter to day and was very glad to hear from you. But why the devil did you not write to me before by gravy! John if you wait so long again I shall raise Hell with you dam if I don't. Well John your letter found me quite well and I hope this will find you the same. I have got back down to Tennessee again and are encamped at Dechard Station. I had a dam good time having furlough but I feel dam good since I got back. I am rite to serve here and am feeling bully ike.[28] I hope [you ain't] ass a-bare and hain't got the shitts neither as you say you hope for. What the devil you want them for John? They [won't] do you any good. Better that than rot away and take good care of your health or you will cave in John. If you don't look out for yourself there is really no one down there to look out for you so take care and don't get sickly John. Now I want to make a bargain with you: I want you to write to me every week. Will you Johnny? . . . Write to me every week write as soon as you get this and tell me all about where you are and what Corps you are in and Brigade and Division and all about the boys. You say that neither has diserted, don't you ever try that John. I have seen five men shot for that and I don't want to see any more. Sticke to your policy [even] if you die a-fighting. Take good care of your self and keep clean and you will come home all write. After all we will have [that drink at] the south line if nothing happens to us. Give my love to all the boys tell John Hen [ry Mattoon] to write to me and Smoke Barnes [too]. I can't think of much more to write so I will close by saying good by John. Write soon and tell me all about everything come what will, or may, Dear Brother.

Charles B. Mattoon Co Y Fifth Conn Vols 1st Brigade 1st Division 12th Army Corps - Dechard Station near Nashville Tenn

Charley's view of desertion, punishment, and honor would come to reflect John's own feelings as he witnessed the event more and more frequently throughout his service. More broadly important was the issue of health that was always on the minds of soldiers during the Civil War. Disease was far and away the biggest killer and medical care was rudimentary. Far more men died of intestinal diseases such as typhoid fever, dysentery and diarrhea than from battle. The main culprits were the filthy conditions and poor diet that characterized camp life for the common soldier.

Sensing rightly that the regiment was going to be on the move, John wrote to Charlotte on April 25th.

Camp Stow
Halltown Va. Apr 25th 1864
Dear Sister

Lot, [seeing] I have not written to you before I guess I will write to you now Before I leave this Camp. We have pulled down half of our tents and tomorrow we start for somewhere I guess. A part of the Regt left here yesterday and the rest will soon fowlow them. The talk is we are going to Spartinsburg But we can't tell any thing about it. Some says we are going then some says we are a-going to the Army of the Potomac so I don't know. I don't know where we will go just as likely to go to Texas as anywhere for what I Know But I don't Care a darn where I go. I had just as like to be in one place as another. Orlando Wariner turned in his horse saddle and every thing he had and has gone off somewhere, we think he's gone to Frederick City to the General Hospital. He is a mean old skunk any way and we were all glad to get rid of him. We heckterd him a most to death poor fellow...

Orlando Wariner, one of the "boys from Canaan" even though he was thirty eight years old, had enlisted in Company A of the 21st New York Cavalry on December 29, 1863, and it was surely from him that John found out that the Regiment was in formation. Apparently he was one of the men who was either not acclimatizing to the life of a soldier, was thought of poorly in his home community or was so annoying to others that he was hounded out. Regimental records are unclear about Wariner, as he is listed by New York State as having been "discharged for disability" on April 8, 1865, in Philadelphia, Pennsylvania of all places, but he is not listed as active on any company roster. It is most likely he spent the rest of his service sick in a hospital as he is not mentioned again by John Mattoon until almost 1866. Lending credence to this interpretation is the statement by Reed in *Tibbit's Boys*; "During the months of March and April, the Griswold Lights had a number of men sick in the hospital at Sandy Hook and back in the Cavalry Depot in Giesboro."[29]

III.   New Market and Early's Washington Raid

The 21st New York Cavalry distinguished themselves in the early months of their service. Unfortunately they would end up on the losing side more often than not, and it was not until President Abraham Lincoln replaced his top generals that the situation began to change.

The Griswold Lights participated in their first major battle on May 15, 1864. Prussian born Gen. Franz Sigel moved up the Shenandoah toward New Market, Virginia with 6,500 men. Sigel was important to the cause as he rallied many German Americans to enlist in the Union Army, but he was considered an inept general.[30] On the way south their rear and flanks were continuously harassed by Mosby's guerillas who disrupted supplies and communications. Sigel's force faced a force of similar numbers under Gen. Breckenridge and Gen. Imboden of the Confederate cavalry. Additionally, 247 Virginia Military Institute cadets commanded by their professor, Lt. Col. Shipp, had been added to the "rebel" lines. These youngsters would play a heroic part in the ensuing battle.[31] Lt. Col. Charles Fitz Simmons of the 21st recalled that prior to the engagement Sigel made extensive use of his cavalry to scout the enemy; so much so that the various parties moving through the rainy forests had trouble identifying who was who and the most serious casualties leading up to the battle resulted from friendly fire.[32]

On the day of the battle, in a heavy afternoon rain, the 21st NY Cavalry were forced by poor positioning on uneven wooded and rocky terrain to charge across a stone bridge at fortified positions. Confederate riflemen met Tibbit's troopers with heavy fire which forced them back in confusion.[33] John Mattoon's beloved horse was shot out from under him in the rout. Two members of his Company L were captured: overall the Regiment suffered thirteen casualties.[34] The Federal positions were overrun and their forces retreated in poor order, falling back to Strasburg. The Federals under Sigel lost 831 men and the Confederates 577.[35] The battle was considered a hard-fought loss due to bad generalship and mismanagement.[36] Subsequently Sigel was relieved of his command and replaced by Major Gen. David Hunter. The published historical literature on the Battle focuses on the west side of the Valley Pike and there is virtually no mention of the 21st New York Cavalry in the engagement.

Whiling away his time back at Camp Stoneman as a dismounted trooper, John Mattoon had plenty of down time to write to his sister Charlotte Bristol about the battle and subsequent events. He described them in a surprisingly matter-of-fact way:

Headquarters June 12th 1864
Camp Stoneman

Dear Sister Lot,
I received your letter last night and was real glad to hear that the folks are all
well. You wrote that you was afraid I was wounded or sick or something else.
There is nothing the matter with me and I will prove it. I will tell you my
history sister since I left Martinsburg [VA]. When we left Martinsburg we
marched to Winchester without any trouble. We stayed there about two weeks
then we packed up and went about 40 miles south and encamped near the
village of Strausburg [Strasburg]. We stayed there 2 days and then we packed
up again and went on about 60 miles farther and stoped near the town of
Woodstock. We stayed there about two weeks a-doing picket and patroll duty
then we picked up our traps again and started off. We started off in the
morning before daylight and marched to New Market. Thare we met the
rebels and fought a battle. Got licked like thunder and had to put back again.
Well, I had my old horse shot out from under me in the fight so I had to foot it
back to a little village called Mount Jackson [The next town north, about 8
miles]. Thare is where we carried all of our wounded men. Well I footed it
back to thare and then I helped carry the wounded into the Church. We stayed
thare till the Regt. came up and then I went to the Captain [Capt. Edward E.
Hedley] and told him that I had my horse shot and asked him how I should get
along. He told me to do the best that I could. Well the Army started on the
retreat on about 10 o'clock at night. I stayed there in Mount Jackson till about
half of the army had gone by, then I jumped on to a piece of artillery and rode
on that all night and in the morning we stoped a little while to get our breakfast.
I filed off of the old piece of artillery and went down to a house and asked for
something to eat and they gave me a bully breakfast. Well if that did not make
me feel good...I eat my breakfast and then went back and bye that time the
Army was on the march and my old artillery wagon had gone on. Well I sit rite
down and waited for another until the wagon train come up then I jumped up
and got in one of them and rode all day. At night we encamped at Strausburg
[Strasburg, about 35 miles north of the battlefield] again. Thare is where I left
the Regt. you see I had no horse and so I was no good there. Well at
Washington the government has a Dismounted Camp where they send all of the
men that get their horses killed or die [of disease]. They send them rite here
and keep them here until they can mount them. Well I left the Regt. the next
morning for Martinsburg with about 100 more dismounted men from our and
other dismounted regts. We went with a wagon train and nothing worth telling
occurred. We arrived at Martinsburg all rite then we took the [railroad] cars
and went to Harpers Ferry. From Harpers Ferry we came here and have been
here ever since. So you see there is nothing the matter with me, so you need
not worry. I am all rite and feeling first rate but I guess I have written enough
about that....

John's first major battle did not seem to faze him much. He could have been
captured on the field, as two of his company had been, but he chose to follow his
regiment off the field on foot. His individual resourcefulness and tenacity in

rejoining his Company and subsequent disgust at having to leave it again speak volumes about his burgeoning sense of duty and his deep interest in being a cavalryman.

Life as a dismounted trooper in Camp Stoneman must have been boring and demoralizing for John. After just two months on active duty, he found himself immobilized while waiting to procure a new mount. He was still with his Regiment, as Camp Stoneman was the base headquarters and rear echelon for the 21st New York Cavalry. While the Regiment continued to fight in and around Staunton in a series of skirmishes and one pitched battle, a Union victory on June 5, 1864 at Piedmont, VA, John Mattoon sat out the fighting and continued to write letters:

Headquarters
May 22 1864
Camp Stoneman
Cavalry Division
Army of Western Virginia

Brother Horace

[Seeing as] I have a little time I will improve it by writing to you. I am well at present and hope this will find you and all the folks the same. Well I have got back as you see to Camp Stoneman again and the devill only knows when I will get away from here again. I hain't got any money or any tobacco or anything else. When you write I want you to put a chew of tobacco in the letter and send it along for I am almost dead. I hain't had a chew in about 3 or 4 weeks. I left the fort about 9 weeks ago and went to Martinsburg then went to Harpers Ferry and from the ferry I came here. I guess I will stay here for the next 3 or 4 months but I wish not. I would 10 times rather be with the boys! At the front I had my old HD shot at the Battle of New Market and I hain't had any horse since. I wish I had your old bay - perhaps you had better box him up and send him down. There is no news to write that I know of only the boys was all well when I left [the] Roost. When you write to me I want you to direct to:

Edgar P Holdridge
General Hospital
Camp Stoneman
Washington DC

He has been here in the hospital ever since last spring and you must not put on the number of my post or the letters of my Company for if you do it will go to the Front I cant write any more now I will dry up

John E Mattoon

Twenty-one-year-old Edgar Holdridge had enlisted at Aneram, NY on January 14, 1864. He was assigned to John's Company L but grew ill in the spring and apparently never got well enough to fight. John surely visited him frequently and as a "resident" of the hospital rather than a transient in Camp, Edgar's more permanent address was a welcome help in securing letters from home. Pvt. Edgar Holdridge is listed as "dying of disease" at Camp Stoneman on July 23, 1864.[37]

By June, John Mattoon had little to write about except his keen desire to get back into the fighting. On the Sixth he wrote Annie: "I ain't doing anything in particular now only laying around camp. O how I wish I could get back to the Regt. I would rather be thare than here doing nothing."[38] This was not the attitude of what many historians have described as very poor quality soldiers that constituted draft or bounty-filled regiments in the latter years of the War. John Mattoon was showing the first tendencies of what later could be called a real sense of duty. It also shows that another of historian Gerald Linderman's concepts, that of "courage" as the glue that held together the common soldier does not necessarily fit in with the actions of John Mattoon, who exhibited remarkable courage throughout the War, yet took it completely for granted, never bothering to mention it in himself or others. He also continued to exhibit a yearning for adventure and excitement which he never lost. Historian Pete Mazlowski in "A Study of Morale in Civil War Soldiers" (2002) placed significant weight on this trait as central to the makeup of a quality soldier.[39]

It is unclear when John was able to return to his regiment. Up until the tenth of June the 21st New York was involved in operations in and around Staunton. After that, the focal point of the regiment's operations became the areas around Lynchburg in and around the Blue Ridge Mountains as part of the newly reconstituted Army of West Virginia under Gen. Hunter. Soundly beaten in a series of engagements with the rebels, the majority of this force was obliged to retreat to Charleston. It is entirely likely that John Mattoon followed Capt. James Graham when he left Camp Stoneman in July as part of a fifteen hundred man cavalry reinforcement brigade from the training facility.[40] This seems even more likely as John reported to Annie on July 31 as having been in the Battle of Bunker Hill, West Virginia which took place on July 2–4.

Bunker Hill was a farming community located south of Martinsburg. Little more than a partially destroyed hamlet on a hill, it was the scene of a cavalry charge by the Confederates under Gen. Gilmore. The 21st New York was dismounted, guarding the ford at Mill Creek below the town (described by John Mattoon as "Ahfords Ford"). A direct cavalry charge against them left one trooper dead, one mortally wounded and four captured.[41] After another fight at Buckletown (or Darkesville) West Virginia, in which the regiment lost three killed, three wounded and five captured, the main body of the Griswold Lights retreated through Harper's Ferry and ended up in camp near Sandy Hook.[42] During this period Harper's Ferry repeatedly changed hands as Confederate

Gen. Jubal Early, (Commander, II Corps) executed an offensive aimed at Washington, backed up by Gilmore's cavalry.

Reconnaissance duty, skirmishes and more casualties ensued for the 21st until Tibbit's First Brigade was assigned to protect an infantry brigade under a French veteran of the Crimean War and the Italo-Austrian war of 1859, Brig. Gen. Alfred N.A. Duffie. A battle took place around Snicker's Gap on 17–19 July in blazing heat.[43] Constant action culminated in Federal troops charging across the Shenandoah River to attack Confederate positions in Ashby's Gap on the afternoon of July 19. The 21st encountered "the combined fire of several thousand muskets and six cannon, the entire force of Confederate Cavalry commanded by Gen. Imboden."[44] In this gallant but futile charge, one out of five men (forty two all told) were killed or wounded. The regiment lost Col. Fitz Simmons to wounds and over half of its other officers. Duffie failed to cross the river, and the 21st was ordered to remain as pickets to keep an eye on the Confederates in line of battle near Ashby's Ford. There were few rations, many troopers had lost their mounts and all were low on ammunition. In his dispatches Duffie hailed the 21st for its conduct in this fierce action.[45] Their heroism was recognized much later when Sergeant Edward E. Dodds, of Company C was awarded the Medal of Honor in 1896 for his actions that day.[46]

This was not the end of the bitter fighting for the 21st New York. On July 21st, they moved back toward Snicker's Gap and prepared to chase Gen. Early's forces toward Winchester. Before that could happen, Gen. Crook's VIII Corps was attacked by Early in the Second Battle of Winchester, (or the battle for Kernstown) on July 24th, the Griswold Lights lost even more men in multiple engagements as they were "driven in confusion toward Bunker Hill."[47] Two cavalrymen were killed, twenty six were wounded, and fifteen were captured or reported missing in action.[48]

John Mattoon participated in the briefly successful counter-charge at Winchester that slowed the advance of the Confederate cavalry at a huge cost in men and horses. John's sergeant, John Mason of Company L was wounded at Kernstown, four of his fellow troopers were killed or reported missing and his corporal, Michael Harrington subsequently died of his wounds on August 12th.[49]

Harpers Ferry
July 31st 1864

Dear Sister

I have a few minutes so I will drop a few lines to you to let you know I am still alive and well. I wrote a letter to Charley yesterday and am writing to you today. Well Ann I have been in some pretty hard fighting since last you heard from me. I was in the battle last Sunday up to Winchester. Ann I never expected to come out alive but I did. We lost 24 men of Company L[50] so the Rebs licked us like thunder. They made us skedaddle back to Harpers Ferry in a hurry. But we are preparing to march up the Shenandoah Valley again and this time we whip the Rebs you can bet high on that Ann. I hain't had a letter from you in ever so long I want you to write to me just as soon as you get this tell Jo[seph] Haight that I got his letter with his picture in it. Tell him I am very much obliged to him for it. I like to see my old friends once in a while tell Jane and Minnie and Charley that I want theirs just as soon as they are taken. Be shure and tell her and be shure and have her send them for I want to see how they all look. I got my state bounty the other day and it is in a Cheque of $50. I will send it home just as quick as I have an opportunity. There is no news to report that I know of I have been in 6 battles since I inlisted and have come out all rite yet. I was in the Battle of New Market, the Battle of Bunkers Hill, the Battle of Ahfords Ford, the Battle of Snickers Gap, the Battle of Pereshville and in the Battle of Winchester. I can't write any more so I will stop.

From John.

John was not downhearted or filled with fear of future engagements. In fact he was sure that soon, "...this time we whip the Rebs you can bet high on that Ann". It seems highly unusual in a man who had seen much defeat and only a few scattered victories. The 21st New York Cavalry was by this time worn down and severely below strength. The men were suffering from fatigue and hunger, the horses were in dreadful shape, and over twenty eight men had deserted, with nineteen others stricken from the rolls for disease or other dischargeable causes. This meant that the Regiment had available for service only about forty five percent of its original one thousand men.[51] Yet they would receive no rest because they were desperately needed to perform picket and reconnaissance duty for almost another month. Finally, on August 24, 1864 they were ordered to dismount camp at Cumberland, Maryland for remounts and additional manpower.

Another fighting man, Sgt. Thomas W. Smith of the 6th Pennsylvania Cavalry wrote home often during his service. The summer battles of 1864 had decimated his regiment as well, and writing from Culpepper, Virginia on May 4, 1864 he mused: "I do not think that there will be much cavalry Fighting in the coming campaign. As our cavalry was never in such poor condition as it is at Pressent. Our Horses are the most miserable looking Kanks, that you ever laid eyes on, and only Half of the men mounted at that. Our Regiment has only two Hundred and twenty five men mounted."[52]

The fighting in the Shenandoah Valley had been far from decisive, and in many circles in Washington it was deemed a disaster. Politicians demanded answers on how to stop Confederate incursions into the North. As a direct result of Gen. Jubal Early's depredations in his attempt on Washington, Federal authorities created the Middle Military Division and Ulysses S. Grant gave it to an intrepid young cavalry commander, Maj. General Philip Henry Sheridan.[53] "Little Phil" took command on August 7, 1864 (with Gen. Hunter immediately resigning) and the Union prosecution of the War in the Valley was about to change dramatically and decisively.

Notes

1.	Thomas James Reed. *Tibbits' Boys: A History of the 21st New York Cavalry.* (Lanham, MD: University Press of America, 1997), 37
2.	John E. Mattoon to Annie Mattoon Stone, *Mattoon Letters,* (July 31, 1864)
3.	William F. Fox. *Regimental Losses in the American Civil War 1861-1865.* (Albany, NY: Albany Publishing Company, 1889), XII, 441
4.	Reed, 45
5.	Fox, VII var. 121-32
6.	*John E. Mattoon Service Record.* New York State Archives, (Albany, NY). 1386-7
7.	Reed, 43
8.	Ibid., 300
9.	John C. Bonnell Jr. *Sabres in the Shenandoah: The 21st New York Cavalry: 1863–1866.* (Shippensburg, PA: White Mane Publishing, 1996), 2. Throughout this book for purposes of investigation and research the author will use the Regimental Roster of the 21st NY compiled by John C. Bonnell Jr. in *Sabres,* which I believe to be the best documented roll of the Regiment. It encompasses a blend of information from The New York State *Adjutant General's Report of 1894*; The New York State *Adjutant General's Muster-in-Rolls of 1867*; Phisterer, *New York in the War of the Rebellion, Vol. 2,* 1053; and the National Archives, *Microfilm Series M 551, M594.*)
10.	Reed, 46
11.	*Richard Arthur to Mother* (September 28, 1863) Richard Arthur Letters. *1863–1870.* Auburn University Special Collections & Archives Department, RG 507.Collection of Auburn University.
12.	Pvt. George Smith was from New Lebanon, NY just north of Canaan. He was 18 and was later taken a prisoner of war at Snicker's Gap VA, on July 17, 1864. Somehow he returned to the Regiment in March of 1865, and remained until mustered out as a Corporal with John Mattoon on June 26, 1866 at Denver, Colorado Territory. Bonnell, 327; Reed 287
13.	Bonnell, 3 cit. Rodenbough, *The Cavalry.* 328. Note that Reed on page 48 indicates that by February, 1864 Geisboro could accommodate up to 30,000 horses, which does not mean that there were that many at any one time.
14.	Stephen Z. Starr. *The Union Cavalry in the Civil War; Volume II, the War in the East from Gettyburg to Appomattox.* (Baton Rouge and London: Louisiana State University Press, 1981), 1–9, 19
15.	Bonnell, 3
16.	Boatner, 108
17.	Reed, 74
18.	Randy Steffen. *The Horse Soldier 1851–1880: The Frontier, the Mexican War, the Civil War, the Indian Wars.* Vol. 2. (Norman, OK: University of Oklahoma, 1992), 86–89
19.	Ibid., 51

20. Bonnell, 4
21. Boatner, 822
22. Bonnell, 4
23. John E. Mattoon to Annie Mattoon Stone, Mattoon Letters, (October 18, 1864)
24. Bonnell, 5
25. Reed, 66
26. *Troy* [New York] *Daily Times.* (25 January 1864), 1, Col. 6
27. Ibid., 73
28. Charley Mattoon served with the 9th Sharpshooters, 5th Connecticut Infantry, Co. Y. Charley fought in such battles as Cedar Mountain, VA, Chancellorsville, and on Culp's Hill at Gettysburg. He had just reenlisted as a veteran "for the duration" after his furlough that March of 1864. It can rightly be said that the hundreds of thousands that re-enlisted won the Civil War for the Union. On July 19, 1865 the Fifth CT Regiment of Veteran Volunteers was mustered out after four years of extensive service including 24 battles and 875 casualties. See a online history of the 5th at http://www.n-ssa.org/NEWENG/5thCVI/ orig5thhis.htm_ for more information on that unit.
29. Reed, 85
30. Boatner, 761
31. Ibid., 588
32. Bonnell, 50
33. Ibid., 57
34. Ibid., 58; cit. State of New York, *Annual Report*, (Vol. 5, 1866) 252, 270, 294
35. Boatner, 588
36. Reed, 63
37. Bonnell, "Roster of the 21st Cavalry", 324
38. John E. Mattoon to Annie Mattoon Stone, Mattoon Letters, (June 6, 1864)
39. Pete Mazlowski. "A Study of Morale in Civil War Soldiers", in Martin Barton and Larry M. Logue (eds.) *The Civil War Soldier: A Historical Reader.* (New York: NYU Press, 2002), 315–16
40. Bonnell, 102–3
41. Ibid., 103
42. Reed, 178; Bonnell, 105
43. Reed, 181
44. Ibid., 183
45. Ibid., 188, cit. O.R. I:37: 320–1, Report of Brig. Gen. Duffie.
46. Bonnell, 119
47. Boatner, 456
48. Reed, 189, cit. Appendix 1
49. Bonnell, 126; Reed, 290
50. This figure is not backed up by official lists, although John may have provided a current list of stragglers, the wounded and dismounts.
51. Bonnell, 128
52. Eric J. Wittenberg. *We Have It Damn Hard Out Here: The Civil War Letters of Sergeant Thomas W. Smith, 6th Pennsylvania Cavalry.* (Kent, OH: Kent State University Press, 1999), 120
53. Boatner, 743–48

CHAPTER THREE

The fact that a man was present at a battle does not imply necessarily that he knows much about it . . . The individual combatant is perhaps confined to a very limited space, buried in smoke, and all the energies of his soul so concentrated upon the claims of each moment, that he has no opportunity for observation.

John S. C. Abbott, 1863 [1]

I.   Remount Camp Again

In late August John Mattoon was once again in Remount Camp. This time however, he was with most of his regiment and taking a well-earned rest. Many of the regiment's officers were not in attendance, having been furloughed home to upstate New York in shifts. The troopers had turned in their horses and were stationed periodically as un-mounted pickets guarding the Baltimore & Ohio Railroad in Cumberland, Maryland.[2] There the bulk of the regiment would sit, gazing across the North Branch of the Potomac River, until November 7, 1864, when they finally received new horses and replacement carbines. The camp was near the edge of town, and as such camps were often very similar, the description offered by Charles Gardner, of Company A, 1st Maine Cavalry is useful:

A square piece of land was selected by our engineer, large enough for 12 companies and 12 streets running through parallel to each other, wide enough for our tents or cabins and our horses. The horses were kept in front and the street between us and the horses was probably 12 to 15 feet wide. We set posts into the ground about 15 feet apart and 3 ½ feet high. These posts extended the whole length of the Company and our horses were hitched to them with ropes . . . We built our cabins of small logs . . . our chimneys out of split sticks and clay mixed with water. When we could get canvas and wood we used them for roofs. Bunks were on one side, and we had two blankets and our overcoats.[3]

After the Camp was built by the men of the 21st, they speculated about probable free time and hatched various schemes to avoid General Duffie's standing camp orders and the guards that prevented them from going into town.[4] There were numerous attempts to sneak out of camp, and the provost marshal and the military police had great difficulty trying to find all the men who walked out of camp without passes. As a result there were many men in the guard house or on punishment drill.[5]

Idle hours were spent writing letters and reading. "*Harpers Weekly* and *Frank Leslie's Illustrated Newspaper* were by far the most popular pictorial newspapers in the Union ranks while the *American Review* and *Atlantic* were the most widely read magazines."[6] Physical activities such as boxing, running races, and baseball were popular. Fireplace discussions were a constant source of information and exchange of ideas. Teasing and practical jokes were also common.[7] Food and tobacco were continuously on soldiers' minds as well. John Mattoon rarely failed to ask his brothers-in-law from home for a "chew" in his letters. John apparently did not smoke a pipe, or indulge in cigars, the more expensive habit of most Union officers. The seamier side of camp life was also firmly entrenched in and around the Army of the Potomac, especially after pay day. Frequent swearing, drunkenness and gambling were "escape vehicles from both horror and loneliness", combating the "struggle with boredom."[8]

Prostitution was omnipresent although harder to access in camp. Camp followers and visiting ladies were discouraged as much as possible yet were still often available, often following paymasters to regiments. The big capital cities like Washington D.C. and Richmond, Virginia were overflowing with thousands of women for hire. It was a matter of life or death for some women, for others it was purely economic. For whatever reason, thousands of prostitutes earned substantial sums while risking their health and even their lives during the war.[9]

Camp life at Cumberland must have been fairly boring to the men of the 21st. Although they were purposely kept busy by the remaining officers in an attempt to keep them out of trouble, the routine must have degenerated substantially with the absence of horses in the command. The regiment's standing orders set the daily routine while in garrison:

4:45 a.m.	Bugler's Call
5:00 a.m.	Reveille, Assembly and Roll Call
5:30 a.m.	Stable Call (Feed horses with hay)
6:00 a.m.	Recall
7:00 a.m.	Sick Call
7-9:00 a.m.	Bugler practice and Company Duty
9:00 a.m.	Watering Call
10:00 a.m.	Guard Mount

11-12:00 p.m.	Drill
12:00 p.m.	Recall and Dinner
12:45-3:00 p.m.	Drill on Horseback
3:00 p.m.	Watering Call, then Stable Call
4:00 p.m.	Recall
4:30 p.m.	Assembly and Dress Parade
6:00 p.m.	Supper
6:45 p.m.	Stable Call
7:30 p.m.	Bugler's Call, Tattoo, Assembly
8:00 p.m.	Taps[10]

A note on officers and non-commissioned officers might be helpful in understanding camp life as well. The recruiting process itself created issues that would only partially recede in combat. Colonels Tibbits and Fitz Simmons and a few other officers and men were respected veterans, but many others were well known in local communities and did not command any great respect until they were proven in battle. Oftentimes they were objects of complete derision. If they could show courage and keep their men from dying too quickly, they were worth some respect. However in camp the situation often deteriorated. Volunteer officers often did not provide the firm discipline that was needed (such as that enforced on the march with other regiments present). The resulting opportunity to do almost anything but routine camp discipline certainly was taken advantage of by the common soldier. In all of his letters John Mattoon never mentioned his officers either negatively or positively. By all accounts, Col. Tibbits and Lt. Col. Fitz Simmons were very good military leaders and kept the regiment reasonably well run and fed by the standards of the day, but that meant little to the common soldier who looked on any deprivation as the direct fault of his officers.

II. The Hard Men

When a large group of men sat idle in camp for an extended period and then received a visit from the paymaster, the result was often an outbreak of riot and lawlessness. "Mutiny and threats of murder were not usual discipline problems. Straggling, drunkenness, fighting, dereliction of duty, theft, desertion, malingering, cowardice, bounty jumping, and insubordination were the common fare at courts-martial."[11]

According to historian Bell Wiley, "probably the most common of all offenses was absence without leave."[12] Every regiment had a group of particularly hard cases and the 21st New York had their share. Military courts (a board of three or more officers brought together to try a case) existed on both sides in the Civil War, but were used sparingly due to time constraints and an inability to get officers together. Justice was most often meted out by commanding officers in the form of corporal punishment, fines, extra duty, and reduction of rank.

Spying, murder, cowardice, desertion, theft, and bounty jumping drew especially harsh retribution in the form of branding or execution by firing squad. Enlisted men received quick and often brutal punishment. Officers, on the other hand, while indeed frequently arrested during the Civil War for a variety of offences, rarely faced more than fines, house arrest, or reassignment. The disgrace of a high crime usually required the officer resign his commission.

The gulf between the officer corps and the enlisted man was very real and very large. Often it seemed the two groups came from different worlds, particularly to the families of officers who were allowed to witness events firsthand.

Even to the educated wives of officers the punishments seemed needed. Ellen McGowan Biddle in her 1907 memoir, *Reminiscences of a Soldier's Wife*, recounted such events from her point of view and remarked on the perpetrators. Her husband, Colonel Biddle, was in command of the Eleventh Infantry just after the end of the Civil War when he was made aware of two bullies who "had knocked down and hurt a couple of peaceful men." "The next morning the Colonel made them walk the earthworks in a barrel with the head and bottom knocked out and a heavy log of wood across their shoulders...drastic measures had to be used in those days. The men, both foreign and domestic were a hard set; not at all the class of men we now have in the army."[13] Punishments that involved this and many other forms of community shaming were used by most regiments.

Mutinous acts were common during the Civil War and unless they were large scale events they were often swept under the rug as quickly as possible by the officer corps, who had no interest in being court-martialed. Such instances occurred throughout the War, and "collectively they had a profound impact. Tens of thousands of men fought for months or years, not for cause and country, but to escape quick death or long imprisonment."[14]

While most of his comrades accepted dismounted camp life and the general boredom, John Mattoon decided to act on information that his cousin and friend Benjamin Francis "Frank" Mattoon, son of his Uncle Ben of Canaan, New York was nearby with his regiment, the 159th New York Infantry. The 159th had spent most of 1863 in Louisiana. Recently Frank was assigned to the 19th Army Corps that was part of the Army of the Shenandoah, now commanded by Maj. Gen. Philip Sheridan. John grew up with Frank and had kept up with him in 1859 when he was a resident of Rocky Hill, Connecticut while John was working as a farm laborer in Wethersfield. John very much looked forward to seeing him again and decided to take some "French leave" or go AWOL (absent without leave). He recounted what happened next in a remarkable letter to Horace Crocker Bristol (Charlotte's husband):

Headquarters
1st Brigade 1st Cavalry Division 8 Army Corps
21st Regt NY Cavalry

Company L
Aug. 27th 1864

Brother

I thought that I would write to you once more. I have had a few adventures perhaps you have not heard of, I will relate a little adventure I had the other night when I went to see Frank Mattoon. I started from camp about 6 1/2 o'clock and went to Harpers Ferry. Well I went to cross the pontoon Bridge when Halt! was the first thing I heard. Well I stopped when a guard came up to me and asked me if I had a pass. No sir! I says. He says you can't get across the bridge then. All rite then, so I turned around and went down the river a little ways and striped myself stark naked, put my clothes on my head and forded the river. Well I got across all rite I put on my clothes and started up town. I had not gone far when Halt! I had brought up a guard - have you got a pass? No sir! Corporal of the guard! he yells - next thing he yelled at me. I know the rest would be thare and I would soon be in the guard house. Well I had a club in my hands that weighed about 4 pounds thinks I, boy you and I will have a tussel before the Corporal gets here so says I. Here comes the Corporal and he partly turned around and I give him a whack over the head with my club that laid him out on the ground rite smart. Well I turned around and the Corporal was a coming I started to run up the road and the Corporal after me. He got to where the guard lay on the ground and he stopped. Well I didn't wait much I went down the river bank, I went about a half of a mile and them I stopped to sit down to rest and think what to do next. Well pretty soon I started on. I went a little farther and was halted again well this time I didn't stop by a long shot I went on the run and I hadn't gone a great way and Blam! went a bullet past my head an I went prancing away like a smart bull. Well I went on and inquired for the 19th Army Corps. I found that all rite and then I found Frank and stayed with them all rite and part of the next day and then I went back to camp. I had a good many hard times coming back but I can't write any more now. Give my love to Lot and kiss Claude[15] for me. Yours from John

Write to me just as soon as you can and send me a chaw of tobaco.

At the time John paid his illicit visit to Frank, the 159th New York was near Halltown, Virginia (now West Virginia) a hamlet about four miles southwest of Harper's Ferry, the scene of heavy fighting on August 14, 23, and 24. They were also stationed near Charlestown, West Virginia on August 21 and 22.[16] These places were roughly ninety-six miles from Cumberland, Maryland. John could not have traveled these distances on foot. Yet he described walking to Harper's Ferry and fording the Potomac River, which suggests his trip to visit Cousin Frank could have only been a dozen miles at most. It thus stands to reason that John found himself at Harper's Ferry or Camp Stoneman on some detached duty from the Regiment in Cumberland and used that opportunity away from his officers to visit Frank Mattoon, who was close by.

Charles Gardiner in *Three Years in the Cavalry* described how sentry and picket duty worked on the Rappahannock; John Mattoon would have come up against a similar system on the Potomac:

> Each relief usually stood two hours on and four hours off...thus we were lined up along the river usually at ¼ to ½ mile apart at regular appointed posts. We would walk our horses up and down the length of our so called beats and each post was numbered, 1, 2, 3, as the case might be. Our orders were very strict. No one was allowed to approach us to within a certain distance without the countersign, not even the relief and it was the only time and place where a private soldier could command a commissioned officer".[17]

There isn't any question that the common enlisted man in the Union Army during the Civil War was hard and unyielding. We are indebted to John Mattoon for an understanding of the enlisted men who stayed and fought: they were not angels. John was a sixth-generation American and men of his farmer/warrior class more often than not tried to emulate the ideal of President Andrew Jackson (1767–1845). "Old Hickory" was worthy of emulation because he was a hard, self-made, capable, self-reliant individual who espoused populist political leanings. These men strongly adhered to the ideology of free labor and working for oneself without any help from any other person. The disillusionment accompanying the industrial revolution and its class of permanent wage earners had not yet set in for this group. "Such men often rejected military standards and discipline, selected officers for almost any but military reasons, pursued state and local interest at the expense of the national."[18] This enlisted man was "a real democrat, conscious of his democratic rights, and resentful of military interference with his freedom as an American citizen."[19] Much has been made of the assertion that these were traits exhibited by many Confederate soldiers and much less so by the Union Army soldiers. However there can be no doubt that this individual spirit lived on in the foothills of Columbia County, New York and elsewhere in the Union ranks as well. His general attitude and demeanor as witnessed by the letter above leave little doubt as to why John was never made a corporal.

The tone of John's letter recalling his absence without leave "adventure" to see Frank leaves no doubt that he matter-of-factly believed that this activity was business as usual for an enlisted private. There is no regimental record of John Mattoon ever having been listed as being absent without leave, as having deserted or even as having been punished for his activities. This was not uncommon as officers did not want to draw attention to incidents that reflected poorly on themselves. It is more than likely that he did indeed get punishment in some form, although the duration of his absence would indicate it was probably light as long as the charge of assault was never found out, which it apparently was not.

There is a certain mystery in John Mattoon's continued service to his country. On the one hand he had proved himself to be an individualist from his early teens; on the other, his decision to join the Army must have reflected his readiness to subordinate his own interests for those of his country. What led him into the cavalry? It was almost certainly not patriotism, because as mentioned earlier, the bounty money was the precipitating factor. Another motive was the likely alternative to cavalry service; the life of a farm laborer. But it could also be said that individual prosecution of the war became more personally fulfilling as friends and family already involved in the conflict still needed new men to provide critical mass to finish the job. Insular farming communities with generations of the same families working the land disposed men to put a high premium on defending family, community, and honor. By the time John Mattoon joined up, the war was by no means over, and his brother and other friends in the Canaan community were fighting and needed help. As the Union effort gathered momentum it seemed to draw men out of their private preoccupations and into the great collective struggle that was taking place. Perhaps the tension between rugged individualism and patriotic duty tended to dissolve as the continued progression of the war and the steady politicization of the slavery issue trumped other social concerns, yet this does not seem to fit in with John's brand of motivation.

The continued disorder at the "Camp near Cumberland" that affected John Mattoon had dire consequences for other men. A man from the 1st New York Veteran Cavalry (encamped with the 21st NY once again) was hanged for murder on October 30, five men were disciplined from the Griswold Lights for drunkenness on September 21, three deserted and there were multiple arrests made by the Cumberland Constable.[20]

During this period the 21st New York missed the battles of Third Winchester (Opequon) and Cedar Creek. These September victories for "Little Phil" Sheridan were the last two large scale pitched battles to be held in the Shenandoah Valley. Cedar Creek in particular was a decisive encounter as it effectively crushed Confederate power in the Shenandoah Valley. After an early morning surprise attack by the Confederates nearly overwhelmed the Federals, Sheridan's celebrated ride through his retreating troops, rallying them to stand and fight with his hat on his sword, eventually swung the battle toward dramatic victory.

Sheridan proved quick and fearless, (the 5' 5" General had risen from the rank of Captain in six months) and older, less motivated officers were rapidly forced out of his command. General Duffie, the Griswold Light's former Division Commander, was reassigned and headed north of Winchester and into obscurity. However, further humiliation awaited him as he was captured by Mosby's guerillas en route home on October 24. This set the tone for the hit and run tactics between the Union cavalry corps and Confederate irregulars that continued to the end of the conflict.[21]

III. An Awakening

John Mattoon was very unhappy that he received so little mail. This was particularly galling as he felt strongly that he was fighting for his family and his community. He believed that "to be a good son, a good brother, a good husband and father, and to be a good citizen meant trying to be a good soldier."[22] Canaan, New York and the Mattoon family knew that John had met and perhaps exceeded expectations as a citizen soldier, and John had made sure in his previous letters that they did. Yet his reward seemed to be the cold shoulder from the folks at home. Reassurance from home was crucial to soldiers, "and painfully missed when letters did not come."[23] "The craving for correspondence was so great that Yanks would entreat, importune and even browbeat folk at home to write and to write fully and often."[24] Mail call was a major event for John as it was for most every soldier in both blue and grey. His letter of the morning of September 13 was one of a number in this period that saw him lapse into resentment and self-pity:

Headquarters
21st NY Cavalry
Company L
2nd Brigade 1st Cavalry Division 8th Corps
Camp Near Cumberland
Sept. 13th 1864

Dear Sister Annie
In answer to yours, which I received in due time, I write this letter. Myself as well as all the boys from Canaan at the present time are well. Now Ann I want you to write to me oftener than what you do all together, for I don't get a letter from you once in a chip bird's age. I want you to write to me 3 times a week regular then I can hear from home often enough to suit me. I will answer all your letters. A good many of the folks in Canaan that I thought was my family had proved untrue to me. Many that I thought as much almost of as I wuld of a brother or sister but they don't think enough to John Mattoon to write to him. Anxiously I wait for a letter and when the bugle sounds "fall in" for the mail I am the first one out of my tent waiting for it. My first words to my sergeant: "Is thare any mail for me?" His answer is short and quick: "no sir". Then I can go back to my tent and wait till the next night when we will fall in for our mail again. I ask the sergeant the same question and most always it is that short quick "no sir". Well if none of the folks in Canaan think enough of me to write then they know what to do rite up to the handle...it makes no difference to me. I can go into battle and fight for my country and I can get wounded or perhaps killed, no one cares for that – they will say at home "never mind it is John Mattoon he never was good for any thing, he might as well be dead or alive" All rite. I will live anyway if for no more than to spite them. I can write no

more this time so good bye. If you answer this you can send me a few postage stamps if you please. Yours from a poor good for nothing soldier.

J E Mattoon

Bully ike[25]

This is the first time that John mentioned "for my country" in any letter. It is an awakening of patriotism and nationalism indeed, as he directly linked the welfare of his family and community to the war effort. He angrily complained that Annie and the rest of the family and friends do not see this link and therefore discount his courage and steadfastness through inattention. "Johnny Rebs and Billy Yanks, far from home, displayed the rude strength of youth, but large numbers of them had youth's terrible capacity for loneliness . . . Accentuating that loneliness was a sentimentality characteristic of mid-nineteenth century America."[26]

This sentimentality was in full swing as the realization hit that if the Union were to lose, the country that he knew and was steadily learning more about would no longer exist. That meant that the life that he knew so well in Canaan would be directly affected too. Somewhere in battle, or talking with other soldiers, or even in a newspaper, the kernel was sown and in this letter it finally sprouts. John knew now that he *must* fight. While still certainly not a believer in the "glorious cause" of defeating slavery, John Mattoon was writing to his family of his willingness to die for his beliefs, even if they were not held by them "if for no more than to spite them". The "bounty man" who had been little motivated by ideology of any kind and only partly by honor and duty had found the reason to persevere as a soldier.[27]

Only a day later he wrote his sister Charlotte Bristol a very different letter:

Headquarters
1st Brigade 1st Cavalry Division
8th Army Corp
Camp Near Cumberland
Sept 14th 1864

Dear Sister Lot

I received your letter last night and was very glad to hear from you again I am well and felling Bully Ike. I was very thankfull for that chew of tobacco that Horace sent me for I had had none in a good while. We are having Bully ike times hear, I hope we will stay all winter but I don't think we will for we are a-going to draw horses before long and when we get horses then hurrah for the front! Then hurrah for the fight and get away Rebs! I don't know as I care how soon they mount us again for I [would rather be here than] the front. We are encamped in a very beautifull place on a high hill about a quarter mile from the city of Cumberland. When you answer this letter I want you to write me

Charley's [Charles Mattoon's] directions for I want to write him. I am going down town today just for fun. The old Cournell[28] gave me a pass last night for 24 hours so I am going down town as soon as I get this letter wrote. There is no news of any importance to write that I know of, only the boys from Canaan are all well and feeling first rate. I can't write any more now,
So good bye
Yours from your

Brother John

A Kiss for Claud

John knew perfectly well that he could fall in combat, and he was not above hyperbole. His mercurial spirits must surely have risen as he knew well that a twenty four hour pass to Cumberland, Maryland was an invitation to a town that had grown to bursting providing an adult cornucopia of dance halls, taverns, gambling, prostitutes, free-flowing liquor and all manner of diversions from life in the cavalry.

A month later, John Mattoon finally got his chance to ride out again. Confederate guerillas were thought to be menacing Green Spring Run Station, West Virginia and John rode out with nineteen other men from Company L under Second Lieutenant Charles Benjamin. They were joined by sixty-eight men of the 15th New York under Lieutenant Hatch. They were the first detachment from the 21st to leave Remount Camp. Their assignment was to guard the railroad bridge, blockhouse and other fortifications at Green Spring Run. John's detachment remained there until November First when they repulsed a large guerilla attack on the station, after which they were ordered to rejoin the regiment.[29]

On October 18, John wrote heartfelt letters to both "Annie" and "Lot".

Green Spring Run
Oct 18th 1864

Dear Sister

With much pleasure yours was received, but I was sorry to learn that you have been sick....I don't know how long it will be before I will hear the cannons roar again, but if they are a coming at all I hope they will come before a great while for we are getting rusty for the want of a fight. I am going to picket now and as I sit on my horse I write to you. Before an hour from now I may be in a fight for all last night we expected [the] Rebs. But let them come then call me an old fool for telling you. I have a rifle that I can pick a man off with 500 yards every time and I want to try my luck on a Reb before a great while and I guess a chance will be offered us before many days. Thare is no news to write that I know of only that the Boys from Canaan are all well. Annie I want you to write often when you get able for I love to get a letter from my dear Sister.

Home is where the heart is, is the old saying and my heart is in the Army and if by falling, [my] life would serve my Country, they should have it a dozen times. I can't write any more now so for this time I will bid you good bye from your Brother,

John

P. my love to [Older brother] George [Mattoon] and [Older sister] Mary [Fitch] and a kiss for the baby [Claud]

This letter exhibits John Mattoon's patriotism awakening in full flower and is further proof of his newfound desire to fight for the Union. He had proven his courage in battle. In becoming a man and a soldier John was going through a continuing process of self discovery. In trying to explain to Annie why he was fighting, he makes a direct connection with his home, the army and the nation. The language is even more heartfelt and sentimental than before as he explains to Annie that he now understands that his values are in fact rooted in his home. The love of that home and the desire to protect it from harm and change meant transferring that love to the army and the job at hand: service to his country. The Victorian belief structure that duty was a "binding moral obligation involving reciprocity" was now understood by John Mattoon: he knew that he "had a duty to defend the flag under whose protection [he] had lived."[30]

IV.   Politics

Green Spring Run
Oct 18th 1864

Dear Sister
I received yours of the 18th and I just exactly jumped over a 10 rail fence I was so tickled. Well Lot how is every thing around Canaan now a days – I hope all goes well. Everything is extremely well – Bully down here and I ain't seen a Reb in a week something new for me, and that ain't all neither. Our Regt. Goes 400 for Maclellan [Maj. Gen. George B. McClellan, Ret.] and our Division goes very strong for Little Mac. Bully him hey Lot? Well Lot, I suppose by all accounts you have got the nicest Baby [Sarah Bristol] this side of – whare did I say Lot or I meant the other side of – whare – East. Chatham [NY] or Flat. Brook one or the other no doubt. Bully for you Lot and Bully for your Baby and Bully for Little Mac and Bully for all the good Democrats in Canaan or any whare else and to top off with I will say Bully for me and Bully for every Soldier in the field and Bully for all the Sailors on the ocean. Now Lot I want you to write to me just as soon as you get this for I am anxious to hear from you again, and Lot if you are a mind to you may send me some postage stamps for I can't get any here. There is no news worth writing so I guess I will dry up for this time. Yours from your Brother John,

Direct to J E Mattoon
Detachment 21st NY Cav
Company Se Camped at
Green Spring Run
West Va

my Best Respects to Horace and a Kiss for Frank and the Baby Clancy

General George "Little Mac" McClellan was a charismatic and highly respected figure in the ranks, who had lost his command of the Army through repeated and generally well-justified accusations that his prosecution of the War up to November of 1862, when he was finally forced out by Lincoln, had been dilatory at best. Many militant Republicans in Congress and the Lincoln administration eventually came to suspect not only McClellan's military competence but also his loyalty (though Lincoln himself never lent credence to the darkest of these suspicions). The Army of the Potomac itself worried Republicans to the point that "Congressional leaders met in Washington and canvassed ways of getting more Republican newspapers in the hands of the men and stopping circulation of Democratic ones."[31] While commanding the Army of the Potomac in 1862, he was rumored to be harboring Copperhead and pro-slavery sympathies and perhaps even ambitions of establishing a military dictatorship. General Abner Doubleday went so far as to state; "No man who is an anti-slavery man or an anti-McClellan man can expect decent treatment in that Army".[32] In 1864, having resigned from the Army, McClellan was running against Lincoln as the Democratic candidate for the presidency. "Little Mac" was hampered by a Democratic "Chicago Platform" that demanded an end to the war, even though personally McClellan did not subscribe to this plank. He ended up losing to Lincoln primarily because the dramatic Union victories over Jubal Early in the Shenandoah Valley lifted voters' spirits.[33] The perceived hypocrisy inherent in selling out the slaves to end the war also helped generate renewed support for Lincoln, but would have had little effect on the Union enlisted men, who taken as a whole cared little about slavery pro or con as it did not directly affect them in the prosecution of the War.

John's statement that the regiment "goes 400 for [McClellan] and our Division goes very strong for Little Mac" is fascinating; the Union Army as a whole overwhelmingly chose to reelect Lincoln. As previously mentioned, Col. Will Tibbits was of a stalwart Democratic family, as was John Mattoon and apparently a good part of his regiment. They were of course "War Democrats" and back home in New York the tally for the national election including the nineteen towns of Columbia County showed 5,240 votes for McClellan and 4,872 votes for Lincoln.[34] Men in the 21st idolized McClellan, and "many were convinced he was removed solely because he was a Democrat."[35] In fact, New York State split evenly in 1864 between Democrats and Republicans in the presidential vote. Nationally however, Lincoln received 55.09 percent of the popular vote and almost all of the Electoral College.

Four hundred men accounted for over three-quarters of the depleted Griswold Lights at the time. In his fine book on the 21st New York Cavalry, John Bonnell Jr. stated: "Nearly all the men [of the 21st New York] voted for Lincoln as president" at a New York State mandated polling place in Martinsburg, Virginia on November 4.[36] Bonnell got the polling place correct but the regimental politics wrong. However across all theaters of the war the overwhelming Union soldier vote was indeed three to one for Lincoln. Democratic cries of fraud in the soldier vote were loud. Some states did not allow voting in the field and relied on furloughs or other means to get the soldier vote out. "There was considerable mention in the New York papers of the fraudulent voting of soldiers; a friend of McClellan claimed that bayonets were used to enforce falsification of election returns."[37]

V. The Moral Aspect

The urban educated class and much of the officer corps were steadily buying into the changes wrought by the industrial revolution and had a very different outlook from that of a rural farmer. While most everyone agreed that the Union was fighting to quell a revolt against national authority, uniformity of opinion stopped there. Was the Civil War really being fought to free the slaves? For many in the north the answer was yes, and after Lincoln's Emancipation Proclamation and the light it brought to the question, more joined the bandwagon.

There was a long-standing and large antislavery sentiment in the north yet these feelings were also mixed with a strong brand of racism. Most Northerners did not want slavery to expand into other states or the new territories in the West which they believed should be settled by non-slaveholding whites. A blend of racism and economics was essentially what had kept the Republican Party protecting the institution of slavery in states where it was legal. The politicians of the time knew quite well that most people felt that should slavery actually end, a surge of freedmen would run north and start taking their jobs and usurping their roles in white communities. This worried Lincoln so much that he actually contemplated colonizing the former slaves by shipping them off to some other country. Of course at the time slaves were freeing themselves by running away in record numbers. Such "contrabands" were popping up all over the north by late 1862, so in truth such worries were already becoming moot.

President Lincoln had always viewed freeing the slaves as an individual state issue, not a federal one. However, there were real military considerations in the freeing of enemy slaves to create a destabilizing force in the South and to keep foreign states from entering on the Confederate side. So when it finally was presented in January of 1863, abolitionists generally applauded the

Emancipation Proclamation and it may indeed have changed the moral compasses of some in the North who were wavering on the issue of slavery.

Conservatives, among them many War Democrats, wished for a return to "the status quo ante bellum, thereby protecting the country's precious traditions."[38] Other Democrats went so far as to announce the "new war" to free the blacks and enslave the whites. Both Radical and more main-stream Republicans and many of the upper class and middle class bought into the idea of emancipation even if many were not sure of its legality.[39] There is no question however that around one third of citizens and Union soldiery still had not been convinced. Joseph A. Frank in *With Ballot and Bayonet* (1998) stated that by 1864, "71 percent of the North's soldiers favored freeing the blacks and enlisting them in the war effort."[40] The last piece of that quote is the important part, as soldiers understood that black infantry could be a direct help in shortening the war. But it appears likely that many in the New York 21st Cavalry, who had come across little institutionalized slavery in the Shenandoah Valley, and who had probably had read little on the subject, simply did not view it with enough gravity to have it on their conscious minds.

Given the almost messianic tidal wave felt in some circles in the North, John Mattoon never once in any of his letters mentioned blacks, slavery or emancipation. It is as if this widespread moral awakening simply did not register with him. A product of his times and of those social mores, John surely was not without empathy, but it seemed reserved for family and friends only.

VI.   Back to War

Col. Will Tibbits arrived in mid-October 1864 to take command of the 21st again, and on October 22 the Regiment finally received its Colors over a year late from a forgetful or bumbling populace back in New York State. A stirring oration was given and the Griswold Lights were issued horses, rations and ammunition starting the next day. On October 31, they left for Martinsburg, West Virginia on rail cars. By November 7 they had joined once again with Sheridan near Winchester, Virginia.[41]

General Sheridan's plan was to destroy the Shenandoah Valley's ability to feed the Confederate troops. The Confederate command under Gen. Jubal Early was ready to resist these depredations. The 21st New York Cavalry was now part of Brig. Gen. William Henry "One Eye" Powell's Second Division. Powell had been a very poorly treated prisoner of the Confederates until late January, 1864, and was eager for revenge.[42] He was as ruthless as Sheridan himself, and on November 12 he led a decisive (although relatively small) victory over Gen. Lunsford Lomax at Nineveh, Virginia. The Griswold Lights in the First Brigade showed conspicuous valor in charging into the center of the fray, losing one dead, two wounded and one mortally wounded.[43] From this time on, until early January, 1865, the Regiment would be in constant action. John Mattoon may have been too busy fighting to write letters during this period; in any event no letters he might have written during these months have survived.

The 21st then spent weeks on patrol and foraging duties trying to avoid constant harassment from local independent guerilla groups who would come out at night to pick off stragglers and do whatever else they could do to disrupt Union operations. Another action took place on November 22 at Rude's Hill where in pouring rain, a superior Confederate force pushed Sheridan and the disordered Griswold Lights (with four casualties) back across the Shenandoah River to Woodstock.[44] The day before Thanksgiving, Mosby's guerillas attacked in force near the main encampment at Camp Russell and were repulsed. The New York 21st spent the rest of November scouting in the Valley.

On December 6, fifty men of the 21st New York were "on a scout" toward Ashby's Ferry and were ambushed by elements of Mosby's command at a hamlet called White Post. More than half the men in this detachment were captured and the scout's commander, Lt. Nelson Holcomb, was killed along with three troopers. Another trooper died later and two were wounded. Cpl. George "Smoke" Barnes, Company A, of Canaan, NY, a great friend of both Charley and John Mattoon was wounded in the hip and subsequently discharged.[45]

Administrative changes occurred as well. On November 17, Will Tibbits received a promotion to Brevet Brigadier General of Volunteers. As an early winter descended, Sheridan consolidated his command and made thirty-one-year-old Gen. Alfred Torbert Chief of Cavalry, with twenty-four-year-old Gen. George A. Custer taking a division command. Duffie's division was disbanded and integrated into the others.[46] In the extreme cold of December 23 and 24, Torbert tried an unsuccessful large scale raid on Confederate positions around Gordonsville, Virginia. In that action the Griswold Lights lost a few men to capture and many more to exhaustion and frostbite. The regiment sought permanent camp about two miles east of Winchester, calling it Camp Averell, and prepared for winter.[47]

At this point in the endgame of the war, Colonel John S. Mosby had the only active Confederate command left in the Shenandoah. His 1917 memoir tells the tale:

By December, 1864, the war had practically ceased between the contending armies in the Shenandoah Valley. The greater portion of Early's forces had been transferred to the lines about Petersburg, while Sheridan had taken up his winter quarters at Winchester. My own command, which had been operating against his communications, never went into winter quarters, but kept up a desultory warfare on outposts, supply trains, and detachments. And, although the Southern army had disappeared from his front, these few hundred rangers kept Sheridan's soldiers as busily employed to guard against surprises as when that army confronted them. Unable to exterminate the hostile bands by arms, Sheridan had applied the torch and attempted to drive us from the district in which we operated by destroying everything that could support man or horse. But so far from quelling, his efforts only stimulated the fury of my men. In snow, sleet, and howling storms, through the long watches of the winter nights, his men had to wait for a sleepless enemy to capture or kill them.[48]

There was little to do for a soldier in the winter months. For the first time since mid-October John Mattoon sent out a number of letters:

Camp Near Winchester
Jan 14th 1865

Dear Sister Lotty,
I thought that since I had a little leasure I would improve it by writing to you. I am well at the present and hope this will find you the same. We are having pretty good times now and I hope they will let us rest for a little while for we have [had] it ruff and tumble all the time since we have been in the Shanendoah Valley. I wish they would send us to some other Department for I think this is the stinkiest darn hole they could put us into but it seems that when a Regt gets its name up they won't give it any rest at all. The old 21st has seen more hard fighting than any other single Regt in this Department since it has been in active service and I think it is about time to give us some rest. But there is no rest for the weary and so they will keep us a-going but I guess we will stay here for a month or so for they have ordered is to put up winter quarters and that is a pretty good sign. Well Lot how are you getting along with that little one of yours. I suppose you think a great deal of her...how is Horace a-getting along? Tell him that if he don't write to me before a great while that when I come home, he must Keep his eye skinned for Breakers for I will go rite at him on the charge and haggle him with my saber. Tell him that it is about 9 feet long and if he gets that run through his bread basket it would be apt to spile his appitite for a day or so. And if that don't scare him so he will write to me I don't know. [Of course because he is my employer] I shall have to go to picking up [cow] chips for a living or else go in to some other good business or other. Well Lot, I guess I have written nonsense enough for once so I will dry up for this time. Direct to J E Mattoon 21st NY Cavalry Company L Winchester, West Va. My respects to Horace and a kiss for the baby and be shure and write.
J E Mattoon

send me some postage stamps

John was certainly swelling with pride and confidence on a successful conclusion to the 1864 campaign in the Shenandoah Valley; so much so that he could risk a joke about "haggling" his former employer and brother-in-law Horace Bristol with his saber just to get him to write. It is also worth noting that the "stinkiest darn hole" John mentions was the formerly lush and beautiful breadbasket of the middle-Atlantic states: the newly burned out and virtually destroyed Shenandoah Valley.

On the next day he wrote to Annie; "I have been in the Army for 1 year and I have not seen a sick day yet. 2 years more and my term of service will be out hurrah for a jolly time." His wit shines through, but then in the same letter, after asking for a new pair of boots, John lapsed once again into a bout of Victorian "melancholia" brought on by too much camp life and idle time and not enough action: "I guess that the folks at home have forgotten that there is such a human being on earth as John E. Mattoon and I have got so that I don't expect a letter from home anymore . . . Annie I ain't of much Account any way so if you are busy you don't need to write to me."[49] This mercurial plunge in self esteem illustrates that all of John's misgivings and fears were not quelled yet.

In an effort to keep the men active, and to dissuade Mosby's marauding cavalry, the regimental officers kept up daily drill, inspection of quarters, and camp guard duty in the freezing cold. John objected to the constant niggling demands made of the men of the 21st NY Cavalry.

Jan 28th 1865
Camp Near Winchester

My Dear Dear Sister,
I received your letter last night and was very glad to hear from you again. I received a letter from George [Mattoon] the same time that I got yours. Tell him I will write to him just as quick as I can get out of guard. I have left my post to write this letter to you. I have hardly time to turn around I am on duty so much. I got my box from home in due time and Annie you may bet I have got as nice a pair of boots and gloves – they are just what I needed. I got a letter from Charley Mattoon the other day, he is in Savanna, Ga. His Directions are Chas B Mattoon 5th Regt Conn. Vols. Company "G" 1st Brigade, 1st Division, 20 Army Corps, Savanna, Ga. He is well and enjoying himself first rate But he says he hain't had anything but rice to eat for the last 2 months. Tell Len [youngest brother Lenny Mattoon] to write to me for I like to hear from brother once in a while. Tell him I will write just as quick as I get time. John Hen[ry Mattoon] is well but I supposed you knew that [George "Smoke"] Barnes was wounded before this he was wounded about a month ago in the hip but I guess not seriously....

Rations became a problem for the Union Army in the winter of 1864. Sheridan's scorched-earth ravaging of the Valley together with an unusually cold winter created a severe shortage of food.[50] The paymaster had not appeared since December 31 and John Mattoon had to swap a precious loaf of bread for an envelope and paper to write to his older brother George's wife, Mary. It was a far cry from the times of plenty when he first entered the War. The burning of the Shenandoah had the unintended consequence of slowly starving the remaining Union troops garrisoned in the region. He must have been desperate as he really did not like his oldest brother George much, and from the tone of the letter John wrote, the feeling was reciprocated. He was however the eldest son, and apparently doing quite well for himself.

Camp Averill Near Winchester
Feb 15th 1865

Dear Sister [Sister-in-law Mary Patton Mattoon]

I received your letter sometime ago and I could not answer it till now for I did not have the material to answer it with. I have not got any money and no paper and envelopes. I had to trade off a loaf of bread to get this sheet of paper and envelope to write on and suppose I will have to starve one day to make up for it. All the rations we draw is 1 very small loaf of bread and 3 spoons full of Coffee and a little piece of pork about as big as a potato a day. By golly they are starving us to death by inches now . . . I know you think that I am a great boy and I act like a darn fool. I hate to ask you, but if you will get up a box of eatables and sent to me I will pay you 3 times what it is worth when I get payed off if I ever do . . . well I suppose you have a lot of cider and apples this winter by golly. I would like to come up there and have a good drink of [hard] cider now . . .

On the same day John wrote to Annie, but knew better than to try to get food from the Stones, who had just sent him new boots and gloves.

Camp Near Winchester
Feb 15th 1865

Dear Sister

I received yours of the 10th and was again made easy knowing that you were well. I should of answered it before but I did not have any writing paper or envelopes so you see that I could not answer it until now as usual I am well and kicking and hope this will find you the same I and in my tent all alone to day. John Hen[ry Mattoon] and my other tent mate had to go on picket [duty] this morning so it left me alone in the tent. John Hen had a letter from Thad[51] last night. He is in Savannah, Ga. And he says he has seen Charley Mattoon! I am glad he has found him ain't you? Well Ann I am beginning to think of another Campaign. Only 6 weeks more til the first of April and by that time you will see the old 21st a going up the Shanendoah Valley towards Linchburg and many bloody battles will have to be fought before we get thare. But it has got to be done, so no use of talking. There has been no picket firing here in a good while. Old Cournell Mosby has kept surely quiet along back and he had a-better keep quiet too if he don't want to get hurt – for when we get after him he has to dig I tell you. Well I don't Know what to write that will interest you but I am going to fill up this sheet with something so here goes. How does George and hary get along? Tell him the reason I don't write to him is I haven't got the paper to write with and give him my love. You must answer this letter rite away for I like to hear from home. So no more this time yours truly from your Brother,

John
Direct as Usual

Give us back our old Commander and we will whip the Rebels still,
G.B. McClellan God Bless his name.

The Union Forever

The banner of freedom floats proudly on high
The war cry of freemen goes up to the sky
By the homes that we cherish the hearts that we love
That flag shall wave proudly our Children above

    John E. Mattoon

Most soldiers might have been dreaming of a quick end to the fighting and going home soon, but John was not fooled. He knew that there was much more to do and he decided to show some of his own patriotic feeling by attaching the little war poem that must have caught his fancy. Still missing McClellan after he had been gone from the field for quite some time, John provides interesting insight into the common (Democratic) soldier's continued yearning for his command.

A letter to Annie on February, 18 related a failed scouting expedition in force against Mosby's troops by Capt. Henry E. Snow of Co. A, with one hundred men from the 21st (John Henry Mattoon among them) and another one hundred from other units.[52] The crossing took place at Shepard's Mill Ford and it was disastrous, with a total of one hundred twenty five men captured, wounded or killed from the various Union commands.[53]

Dear Sister

. . . I am well and enjoying myself as well as can be expected for you know that there is very little enjoyment for a soldier especially when he is in the field. John Hen is well but he feels pretty well used up to day as he had to scout last night and he had to cross the Shanendoah river 3 times (and it is very high now) and his horse fell down with him in the river and he got pretty wet. I tell you thare was about 75 men went with him and they took 14 rebels prisoners they had a pretty rough time of it . . .

. . . give my love and best respects to Aunt Delia[54]

Interestingly, John only mentioned the privation of John Henry Mattoon, not the killed, wounded, and prisoners from the engagement. He only counted the prisoners taken by the 21st and related that "they had a pretty rough time of it". Perhaps more remarkable is the assertion that he was "well and enjoying myself."

In this period Col. Tibbits and the 21st led a patrol in force starting March 5, which moved through Strasburg, Virginia. Subsequently another large patrol took place on March 10 around Woodstock, Virginia. It is not known if John participated in these forays. It is certain however, that the waiting around camp on low rations was starting to get to John.

Camp Averill, near Winchester, VA
Feb. 25th 1865

Brother Horrace [Horace Bristol]

As I have not written to you in a good while I thought that I would write now a short letter. I have just got in off of piquet [picket duty] and I don't feel very sharp I tell you, but nevertheless I am going to write well or no. Well Horrace how is every thing in General? All lovely I hope. Everything is all right down here only the sons of bitches don't give us enough to eat that's what's the matter. We had pretty good news here last night we heard that General Sherman had taken Columbia and Charleston SC and that General Terry had taken for Anderson opening a clear road to Willmington but I don't know how true it is. I don't place much dependence on the news that I get here thare is no news that I know of in this Department of any importance only that every thing is lovely. Everything goes on just the same all the while nothing is going on at all. I wish they would do something or else give us more to eat I don't care which. Well Horrace how is Lot and the Baby getting along? All rite I hope. John Hen[ry Mattoon] is well and feeling good he is on Camp Guard to day. Well I don't know what else to write, as Ann says: I am up a stump. We had orders to have our sabers ground from hilt to point I guess that that means business don't you, for we have never had our sabers sharpened at all and they say that it is against the Regulations of war to have them sharpened but that's the orders and I suppose they will have to be by golly. I pity us if the Rebs get any of us and we have sharp sabers for they will kill every one they take there will be no quarter shown there and if we do get taken prisoners we are gone up salt lake for sure. Well Horrace I guess I have wrote enough for once so I will close for this time.

Yours truly, John E. Mattoon

On February 27 John Mattoon wrote to his sister Sarah "Jane" Haight that he thought they were "a-going to move somewhere" as they "had orders to have our sabers ground up sharp and we have drawn 90 rounds of Cartridges and 2 extra horse shoes and that all indicates a march. The prevailing opinion is that we are going around Linchburg [Lynchburg, Virginia] and cut our way through to reinforce Gen Sherman but I don't know how true it is I hope that it will prove false for I don't want to go up there again."[55]

Sabers had been used in the initial charge and in close combat at the commencement of the war but subsequently the much more effective pistol and carbine took their place. It apparently was not at all appropriate to go into battle with sharpened sabers according to John Mattoon. "Records show that fewer than a thousand saber wounds were treated in Federal hospitals during four years of combat. Cavalry commanders also quickly learned to use their horses for swift mobility rather than for direct attacks, bringing their men close to the enemy and dismounting them for combat, with one man in each set of four acting as horse holder."[56]

In this period the Griswold Lights were destined to stay in the Valley at camp when not performing long duty as pickets on horseback. In an early March letter to Annie, John detailed the patrol he just had.

Headquarters
21st NY Cavalry Company L
1st Brigade 2nd Division
Camp Averill Near Winchester
March 8th 1865

Dear Sister,
I received your letter some time ago and on the account of so much hard duty I have not had time to answer it before and as I am in a great hurry now I don't know wether you can read this or not. I am as usual well and happy as a clam and hope this may find you the same. I am very sorry that your feet and hands trouble you so you must do the best that you can and if you want any money just you go to Charley Haight and he will give you some for I wrote to him to find you in all the money that you need. Thare is no news of any importance to write only that I had to get up night Before last and saddle up my horse and go out on a scout. We went to Cedar Creek and there my horse got sick and I had to leave him and walk back 16 miles quite a walk wern't it Annie? But I got back about 10 o'clock last night but I had a hard walk of it I tell you. But such is the duty of a soldier and we have to live up to it. Annie I can't write much more this time for I am in a great hurry but will do better next time. Tell Lot to write to me. Good bye Annie I must close for I have got to go on guard. You must write often for I do love to get a letter from my Sister so no more yours from your Brother John.

P. my Best respects to Aunt Delia and you must write soon and direct as usual

John E Mattoon

Brother-in-law and friend Charley Haight back in Canaan provided much support for John both at home and in the cavalry. The friendships and family links were still strong and holding up. "Aunt" Cordelia Harris, his former employer, must be included on that list as well. And on March 17 in another letter to Annie, John described more of the same type of extended picket duty in miserable weather that pushed even his endurance.

Headquarters
21st New York Cavalry Com
1st Brigade 2nd Cavalry Divn
Camp Averill Near Winchester
March 17th 1865

Dear Sister,

Your letter was received and read but a few minutes ago and I hasten to answer it. I was on Picket last night and I think I never had quite as tough a time in my life. The wind was very hard and rain, well that ain't no name for it, it was a regular flood of water... Well Annie there is no news to write of in particular that I know of we have a great deal of hard duty to do but that is nothing but what a soldier has got to expect at all times. You say that Ames has been firing his cannon I suppose it was something new for you to be close to a Cannon when it was being fired off! Shooting Cannon has gotten to be quite an old story with me and thare is nothing that I had rather see than a good piece of Artillery when they are working it. Now Annie I hardly know what to write I hain't heard from home since I can remember and I have made up my mind not to write home any more they don't answer my letters and that is as good as an invitation to stop writing. I will send you my picture just as quick as I get payed off. You spoke about that picture of yours that you have taken in Pittsfield [Massachusetts] I lost that picture at the Battle of New Market Past Spring. I had it in my coat pocket and I had my coat strapped on my saddle so when my horse got shot I had to leave my coat picture and all. John Hen has gone out on a scout to night he started from Camp about 2 hours ago, I don't know how long he will be out. Annie you said you was getting homesick you must go home and stay a while and make a good long visit and then come back and you will feel more like work you know it ain't in the line of a soldiers duty to get homesick so Annie I have never been homesick yet. It is getting pretty late and I did not sleep a wink last night so I will have to draw my letter to a close and go to bed. May your dreams be pleasant dear Sister and may you wake Bright and happy on the morrow. So no more this time, yours from your ever true Brother John.

Ps. My best respects to Aunt Delia and kindest regards and best wishes to Miss Hobert

John E Mattoon

If there were any doubts that John loved his sister Annie they are certainly dispelled in this letter. Despite his own "hard duty" John had time for moral support and comforting words. He was becoming a man who could be leaned on, and his contact with his family and friends continued to solidify.

On March 20, John had time to sit down and write a long letter to his sister Charlotte Bristol. In it he described Pvt. John Farquer of Company M finding unexploded ordinance on their campground, which was built on top of the scene of the Second Battle of Winchester. Farquer's Service Record stated that he was trying to "diffuse" the shell, but John saw it differently.[57]

Headquarters
21st NY Cavalry, Company L
1st Brigade, 2nd Cavalry Division
Camp near Winchester, March 20th 1865

Dear Sister

Your kind and welcome letter was received on the 18th and I was glad to hear from you once more. I am well as usual and trust that this will find you and Horrace the same. Thare is no news of any account that I know of all the boys from Canaan are well or I might better say John Hen[ry Mattoon] and I, for we are all that's left that went from Canaan for the 21st. We are having a great deal of hard duty to do this winter but as a general thing the Boys are tough and strong as can be. I weigh 162 pounds without my overcoat on. We had an accident happen in camp the other day. You must know that a great deal of hard fighting has been done. The ground is tore up in a great many places and the trees are all cut up and the ground is strewed with shot and unexploded shells and the graves of the poor fellows that have been killed are thick. Some of them are not half covered up. No longer ago than yesterday I was going along through a piece of woods and I came to a sort of a dry ditch and thare lay a dead soldier rite in the ditch with his knapsack, haversack and canteen just as he had fell. His musket lay a few feet from him showing that he died fighting for his country. Sometimes I shudder when I see such sights and think what my fate may be. But the accident I was a-going to tell you about – one of the men in Company M picked up one of the old unexploded shells and sit down on a bag of grain and commenced to pounding the shell with his hatchet and the shell exploded and it tore one of his legs off intirely and tore all of the flesh off his other leg from the upper part of his thigh away down below his knee and it tore off one of his hands and otherwise mangeld him up awfully. It was the awfullest sight that I ever saw and I have seen more than a few dead and wounded men since I have been in the Army. Well Lot I have not got the box yet but I expect it is in Harpers Ferry so that I can send for it when we go down after rations. I guess Charley Haight and Jane are mad at me. I am shure I don't know what I have done to make them mad at me but they are surely mad or they would answer some of my letters. I wrote to Charley yesterday and I am sorry that I wrote such a provoking letter to him for he has always been more than a brother to me but I had a mad fit on and I wrote the letter and sent it before I got glad again. I am sorry I wrote it now but no use of crying over spilt milk. Well Lot I shall have to close my letter and go to bed for it is getting

late. Give my best respects to all the folks and kiss the baby for me. So Dear
Sister good night and may your dreams be pleasant and may you wake Bright
and happy on the morrow. So no more,

Adieu   From your Brother
John E. Mattoon

        Kiss Claudy for me

Graphic depictions of the former battlefields and wounds are rare in John's
letters as he mostly wrote to his sisters of camp life and tried to keep such things
from them. It would appear that as he got more battle hardened he expected it of
Charlotte too. He also poignantly described his discovery of a dead comrade-in-
arms. In reviewing the man's fate however, his first thought was not the horror,
but the peacefulness of the scene and the fact that this unknown had "died
fighting for his country." John at this point in his service might still "shudder"
on occasion, but his rapid dismissal of the vignette speaks volumes about his
lack of morbid interest in his own "fate". Frustration caused by boredom is
perhaps behind the "mad fit" that produced the "provoking letter" to his dear
friend Charley Haight. Some of John's temperamental moods seem directly
related to the amount of letters he received. They likely served as his only way
to gauge the extent of friendship and love shown to him by family and friends.
    The next letter in the record confirms that food distribution (and as always
tobacco) was still a serious problem for the Regiment and that care packages
from home continued to be of major importance.

Headquarters
21st NY Cavalry Company L
1st Brigade 2nd Division
Camp Averill Winchester
March 26th 1865

Dear Sister,

I thought that I would write you a few lines this evening to let you know that I
had received the box. I got it today and I tell you I had a feast and I can go to
bed tonight and say I am not hungry.   I can't write much for I have just come
in off of picket and I am very sleepy. Most every thing was all right but the
beans had spoilt I was sorry for that for I had rather of had them than any thing
else. By golly Lot that tobacco is mighty good but I shall have to thank Horace
for that I suppose. I will write you a good long letter just as soon as I get time I
am so sleepy to night that I can't write much so you will have to excuse me this
time. Tell Horace that the Chewing tobacco is Bully so no more to night a Kiss
for the Baby and my best respects to all. From your Brother

John E Mattoon

Winchester West Va

In a letter to Annie a few days later on March 28, he related the big news story of Pvt. Farquer and the ordinance, along with the fact that:

...there was a tree Blown down the other day[58] and it fell on a tent in Company H and killed 2 more men almost instantly. Then thare was 2 Sergeants one of Company B [1st Sgt. Ranson B. Hultz] and the other out of Company H [Sgt. John H. Van Antwerp] went outside of our pickets the other day and the Rebel Guerillas attacked them and killed them Both. One was shot through the head and the other was shot through the bowels but I guess I have wrote enough about such things. The weather is very fine here now the mud is about all dried up and every thing looks like spring.

Apparently Annie was attempting to match John up with a "Miss Hobert" who had enclosed some flowers in the last letter. John proved that even farmers with basic educations could have good manners and a poetic turn for a phrase:

...those flowers were though faded very beautifull, and I will keep them as a momento of friendship. Tomorrow I shall go on picket again. Often while I sit on my horse all alone I think of you dear Sister and of my friends at home. I long to see you all again but my country before my friends. I hope soon to see the old flag flying proudly over the Rebel Capital. Even as I write the distant roar of heavy Cannon greets my ear our men are firing a salute to Gen. Grant in honor of his last victory. It is getting late and I must get what little sleep I can to night for I will have to be up all night on the next. My thanks to Miss Hobert for her kind wishes and may her life be long and happy as she wished mine to be...

John's evolution from boy to man and from "bounty man" to patriot seemed to be intensifying. "My country before my friends" is a statement of a man who has taught himself a broader, more encompassing ideological interpretation of purpose and duty.

By now the Shenandoah Valley theatre of the War had become a backwater. Sheridan had conquered virtually all Confederate resistance. The men felt more than a little left out, but they celebrated every victory taking place farther south. Gen. Jubal Early's depleted army was smashed for good by Sheridan at Waynesboro, Virginia on March 2 and isolated irregulars were the only forces opposing the 21st now. A few pickets were still being killed by Confederates when they got the chance, but a condition of tense truce hung over much of the Valley. Being in the backwater meant meager rations and little in the way of replacement equipment or uniforms. On April Fools' Day John wrote Annie:

Camp Sullivan
Halltown Apr 1st 1864

Dear Sister Annie
I received yours last night and this morning I hasten to answer it. I am well at present and hope this will find you and all the folks the same. We are encamped about 5 miles away from Harpers Ferry. You spoke about my being in a great deal of danger. Well Annie of course I am in some danger but you know that a soldier is hardly ever out of it But believe me Annie I am enjoying my self first rate and as for the danger I care little for that if death comes let it and that all. I don't borrow any trouble at all when it comes it will be time enough to worry. I have got to on guard to day so I cannot write you as long a letter as I wish I could But I will do Better next time. I sent you those verses when I was in Alexandria and the reason why I did not write was that just as I put my paper out I was ordered on guard and I sealed the envelope rite up and gave it to John Hen[ry Mattoon] to put in the office. Tell jane to send me those shirts just as quick as possible or I am in great need of them I have not got any but the one I have got on and that is the old red one that I got before I left home. I have wore it all the time. I took it off once and washed it and went without any until it got dry and it is all tore to pieces now and I don't know when I can draw any. I can't write any more now for I have got to go on guard so good bye and write soon. Yours from your Brother,
John 1864
All fools day

Send them shirts as quick as convenient
(write soon)

John's fatalistic bravado may have been nothing more than that although it appears heartfelt; but there is no doubt that he had become a professional soldier, neither shirking duty nor seeking it. A shirt washed once in sixteen months illustrates the level of hygiene (and disease) in the Union ranks. It is well known that the Confederate cause had great trouble providing clothing and shoes to its armies but the Union had serious problems too. During much of the war the clothing issued to Union troops was of shoddy manufacture. The cavalry had it a bit better than the infantry because they got pattern uniforms consisting of reinforced pants and shell coats, but the rest was often lacking. From previous letters we learned that John had to get his boots from home unless he had the money to buy them, and now his homemade shirt was finally in tatters. Even late into the war, many Union soldiers were forced to make do without shoes. It was hard to leave anything like extra clothes in camp as they often would be stolen. So whatever a soldier had was worn or strapped to his saddle until it ceased being functional. Bell Wiley related the story of a Yankee who witnessed Abraham Lincoln reviewing his regiment: "those who had overcoats were ordered to put them on, to hide the rags and make him believe that they had jackets".[59]

Richmond fell on April 2 to Ulysses S. Grant[60] and on the third there was a great party in the camp of the Griswold Lights with artillery salutes and horse racing.[61] Soon afterward the 21st was ordered to break winter camp and prepare for the spring offensive. But that was not to be. Robert E. Lee surrendered the Army of Northern Virginia at Appomattox on the 9th and Col. Mosby followed on April 21, only after making sure that General Johnston's Army in North Carolina had followed suit. The 21st New York Cavalry was ordered to Washington the next day.[62]

The Griswold Lights had labored valiantly and John Mattoon had done so in exemplary fashion. The immense collective sigh of relief must have been worth more than any formal recognition or bushels of medals. Never one to shy away from a moment in history, "Little Phil" Sheridan immediately purchased the table that Lee had signed the surrender on for twenty dollars. Passing the baton in a prescient way, he then gave it as a wedding gift to Libby Bacon Custer, the brand-new wife of Brevet General George A. Custer, one of whose commands the 21st would be meeting quite soon.

Notes

1. John S. C. Abbott. *The History of the Civil War in America.* (Springfield, Mass: Gurdon Bill, 1863., Vol. I), vii
2. Bonnell, 136
3. Charles Gardner. *Three Years in the Cavalry.* (Tucson, AZ: Ada Friddell and A Plus Printing, 1909, reprint 1998), 31-2
4. Reed, 199; Bonnell, 137
5. Bonnell, 139
6. James I. Robertson. *Soldiers Blue and Gray.* (Columbia: University of South Carolina Press, 1988), 82
7. Ibid., 92; and see Wiley, 171
8. Ibid., 101
9. A good recent book on the subject is Elizabeth A. Topping's, *What's a Poor Girl to Do? Prostitution in Mid-Nineteenth Century America.* (Gettysburg, PA: Thomas Publications, 2001)
10. Reed, "Notes" 212, cit. *Regimental Endorsement Book 1854-1866*, Twenty-First New York Volunteer Cavalry Regiment Gen. Ord. 17, First Cavalry Division, Cumberland, MD, 5 September, 1864
11. Patricia L. Faust, (ed.) *Historical Times Encyclopedia of the Civil War.* (New York: Harper & Row, Publishers, 1986), 117
12. Wiley, 197
13. Ellen McGowan Biddle. *Reminiscences of a Soldier's Wife.* (Philadelphia: J.B. Lippincott, 1907 reprint Mechanicsburg, PA: Stackpole Books, 2002), 29
14. Webb Garrison. *Mutiny in the Civil War.* (Shippensburg, PA: White Mane Publishing, 2001), 294
15. Sarah Claudia Bristol, born February 24, 1863. Mattoon, 74
16. Phisterer, New York. "Tables", 314
17. Gardiner, 40
18. Henry Steele Commager, (ed.) *The Blue and the Grey.* (New York: Fairfax Press, 1982), xxxvi

19. T. Harry Williams. "Voters in Blue: The Citizen Soldiers of the Civil War". In *Mississippi Valley Historical Review*. (Vol. 3, No. ¾, Sept. 1944), 193
20. Bonnell, 139
21. Reed, 205
22. Mitchell, 25
23. Ibid., 29
24. Wiley, 189
25. Bully Ike meant "Great", "Ready to go!" another wry stab at his sister.
26. Robertson, 110
27. See McPherson, 99-103 (and elsewhere) for a discussion of patriotic motivation.
28. Col. Will Tibbits was not back from furlough yet; it was probably the 1st New York Cavalry's commander.
29. Reed, 205; Bonnell, 144
30. McPherson, 23
31. Williams, *Voters in Blue*, 202
32. Ibid., 193
33. Boatner, 524
34. Ellis, 50
35. Williams, *Voters in Blue*, 195
36. Bonnell, 144
37. Harold Dudley, The Election of 1864. *Mississippi Valley Historical Review*, (Vol. 18, No. 4, Mar. 1932), 516
38. Frank, 59
39. In fact it would not be legal or enforceable until the Thirteenth Amendment to the Constitution was ratified in 1865.
40. Ibid., 67
41. Bonnell, 143-4
42. Reed, 218
43. Bonnell, 148
44. Ibid., 151
45. Reed, 223; Bonnell, 155
46. Ibid., 225
47. Bonnell 161-2; see also Reed, 229
48. John S. Mosby, and Charles W. Russell. (ed.) *The Memoirs of Colonel John S. Mosby*. (Boston: Little, Brown & Co. 1917), 333
49. John E. Mattoon to Annie Mattoon Stone, *Mattoon Letters*, (January 15, 1865)
50. Bonnell, 167
51. Thaddeus H. Mattoon was in the New York 128th Regiment, Co. A. A resident of Canaan, he was another son of Uncle Ben. He was three years older than John E. Mattoon.
52. Bonnell, 168
53. Reed, 233; Bonnell, 172
54. Cordelia Harris, was John's employer in Wethersfield, 1859-61 and it is entirely possible a cousin from his father's generation, although a careful search had not come up with anyone of that name attached to the family.

55. John E. Mattoon to Sarah Jane Mattoon Haight, *Mattoon Letters*, (February 27, 1885)
56. Dee Brown. "Fighting for Time" in *The National Historical Society's The Image of War 1861-1865*, Vol. IV. (Washington, DC: National Historical Society), 110
57. Bonnell, 176, cit. Farquer *RG*. 94, Service Records, New York, *Annual Report*, Vol. 5. 296; and Reed, 235
58. The night of March 21st.
59. Wiley, 61
60. And coincidentally Charley Mattoon and his 5th Connecticut Veteran Volunteer Regiment was there, which also had the distinction of being the first regiment in Atlanta.
61. Bonnell, 177
62. Ibid., 181; Reed, 236

CHAPTER FOUR

I.   Washington and Home?

By early April the roads had dried up enough to finally facilitate movement of men and arms on the highways. After breaking camp and marching out of the Shenandoah Valley for the last time, John Mattoon reported in to his sister Annie from the regiment's new camp at Falls Church, or what he referred to as "Earstream" Virginia.

April 25th 1865

Dear Sister,

Again I have moved. We arrived here yesterday after 3 days hard marching. We pased through the City of Frederick [MD] and Washington [DC]. I don't know how long we shall stay here but I hope not long for I don't like the place at all. We are now in Earstream Virginia and so of course we compose of the army of the Potomac if there be such an Army now. It is very pleasant here today I hope you have such fine weather at home for then I would be sure you are enjoying yourselves. Annie I haven't had a letter from you in over 2 weeks but I suppose you have written and I have not received being on the march. As we have not got any mail I have a ring in my pocket a rebel deserter gave me. It ain't worth much it is maid of hair.[1] Thar is no news of importance that I know of. By next winter we will all be home once more and then hurah for a jolly good time. Your Hen [John Henry Mattoon] is well and sends his love (he says you must write to him). We [had] a slight skirmish the other day with some Guerillas at a place they call Balls Cross Roads.[2]   Well Annie I shall have to dry up for this time. You can always read over half of this for I have written in a great hymn. So no more this time. Yours from your ever true Brother,
John

P. my Compliments and best wishes to miss Hobert

John was still not swayed by those in the Regiment that were sure of immediate discharges for veteran cavalry regiments. His reference that "by next winter we will all be home" indicates John still planned to serve out his three years. John's patriotism was also now exhibiting itself in song – this is the first time that John mentioned a hymn. Unfortunately the hymn John copied does not survive, although it seems likely that its religious nature may have been of less interest to John than any patriotic interest it might have had. For the generally non-religious John Mattoon, to find a hymn worth copying and sending to Annie was not out of character in Victorian America. Finding it in print in an Army encampment was no surprise either, in an era of intense religious revivalism in both the North and South. A few days later on April 28, John again wrote to Annie and described his state of mind regarding the light camp regimen and the assassination of Abraham Lincoln.

Dear Sister,

...we are now camped about 16 miles from Washington [DC] at a little place called Falls Church. It is a beautiful little Village and we have got a very nice camp we have but very little to do here. We come on guard about once in 5 or 6 days so you see that that is very light duty. The talk is through the Regt that we are going home on a 3 months furlough but I don't know how true it is. I hope it is true for I sure would like to go home for a little while...well there is not much going on around here, it grieves me the johnnies are about played out I hope so any way. Old uncle Abraham is dead, he met with an awful fate but I trust that before long his murderer is captured. I would like the fun of putting the rope around his neck and then let the scaffold fall and have him midway between heaven and earth. Yes, by golly I could do that – with a good heart I tell you. We bought some fresh fish yesterday and we had them for Breakfast this morning I tell you they were good. It is seldom that we get any such stuff to eat so when we do get it we lay on for a weeks rations...

"Old uncle Abraham" had indeed died on the morning of April 15, and although a Republican, the President certainly deserved mourning by the Democrats of the Griswold Lights as the winning commander-in-chief and a staunch supporter of the common soldier. At a time when the Union seemed to have been made whole again, his death must have been a deeply emotional disappointment.

John Wilkes Booth and his co-conspirators were being sought by the entire Union Army, although there is no record that the 21st had any hand in the hunt, other than being officially added to Maj. Gen. Christopher C. Auger's list of forces that could be used in the search.[3] John did not know that a day earlier a sister regiment from upstate New York had cornered Booth in a barn on Garrett's farm in Port Royal, Virginia. In the early morning of April 26, 1865 a detachment of twenty six men under the command of Lt. Edward P. Doherty of the 16th New York Cavalry along with other Federal authorities, set the barn on fire. Sgt. Boston Corbett of the 16th saw that Booth was not coming out of the barn and took the initiative against direct orders to take him alive, by shooting Booth through the neck. Booth died three hours later. English-born Sgt. Corbett, who had a long history of mental illness including a prewar self-castration, claimed that "God Almighty directed me" to shoot Booth. He was subsequently exonerated of any wrongdoing. Corbett was last heard of in 1888, when he escaped from the Topeka (Kansas) Asylum for the Insane.

It must have sat rather well with the Griswold Lights that a fellow Empire State regiment had brought Booth to justice. John did get part of his rather ghoulish wish in early July when the rope was indeed put around the necks of four of the conspirators.

Headquarters
21st New York Cavalry Company
Camp Near Falls Church Va
May 3rd 1865

Dear Sister Annie,

Your welcome letter of the 20th was received on the 2nd and rite glad I was to hear from you again. Your letter found me enjoying myself first rate and I hope this will find you the same. Well Annie I guess we are a-going to be payed off once more. We signed the pay rolls last night for 4 months pay and expect to be payed off tomorrow. That is about all the news that I know of at present. I hope to hear that peace is declared for I had much rather be on the march and have a little fighting to do that be laying around Camp without any thing to do but a little guard duty, but the war is over and the fighting is done away with so we will have no more of that kind of sport. The talk is through Camp that we will be discharged in less than 3 months but I rather guess that we won't. I don't care weather they discharge me or not although I would like to come home for a little while first rate, but I don't think I should stay around there a very great while for I had rather be on the go. I talk some of inlisting for the Navy to go as a deck hand then I could see what lays on the other side of the big Pacific pond but I guess I will come home first and see the folks around Canaan and then try the sea besides I want to see Miss Hobert if she is such a good girl as you say she is and such a fast friend of yours. Well Ann what shall I write now? John Hen is well and sends love and that is all I can think of to write this time, so I will close hoping soon to hear from you again. I remain your ever true Brother,
John

P. My Compliments to Miss Hobert

I have another ring like the one I sent you. If it would be accepted I might send it to EE.

In this letter, John again lamented the cessation of hostilities: "We will have no more of that kind of sport". In his previous letter he had bemoaned "it grieves me that the johnnies are about played out."[4] In cavalierly equating war with sport John was clearly parading his mastery of his job as a professional soldier, and not just exhibiting the bravado of a flippant youngster glad to have survived the War. He apparently was so bored that he was even contemplating joining the Navy "as a deck hand, then I could see what lays on the other side of the big Pacific pond". His patriotism unabated, John also exhibited an unabated penchant for adventure. It is astonishing and perhaps unlikely that he didn't "care weather they discharge me or not" and although he certainly would have liked to see home and family again, it appears that at this point he had decided a tranquil life in rural New York would be too tame for him. He must have been one of a very small group of Union veterans who *actually wanted* to stay on. The identity of "EE" remains a mystery.

Camp Near Falls Church
East Va May 9th 1865

Dear Sister,

I received your letter last night and was glad to get a letter from you once more. I hope this will find you well and enjoying yourself as it leaves me. Well Annie there is not much news to write everything is just the same as when you last heard from me. This is a beautifull Camp that we occupy. We are within about ½ a mile of the Village of Falls Church and a very pretty Village it is to. We are going to have a grand review on the 15th all the Armies the most of the Army of the Potomac are here or Camped around Washington and we expect a part of Gen Shermans Army here every day so we will have a Army of about 10000 men. It will make a grand sight I tell you. They are a going to have it on the same ground that General McClennen reviewed his troops in 1861 it is at a place they call Balls Cross roads. I suppose after the review they will commence discharging troops I hope. So any way I had some pictures taken yesterday and of all the pictures you ever see they are the worst but I guess I will send you one such as it is. John Hen is well and sends his love. I hardly know what to write by golly I am up a tree as you say. I don't think I shall inlist again untill after I come home, but as Charley says a peacefull home has no charm for me. I like to be where there is something a-going on and in the Army there is no end of excitement. The Shakers say "to lo lodel lodel lo I love to be a Shaker" and I say the same- I love to be a soldier. To be shure we see very hard times but when we are in Camp we lead a lovely life. I think before the first of August the 21st Regt will be discharged. That is my opinion and so it is with the most of the men and officers throughout the Regt. [Major George V. Boutelle] of our Regt bet 1000 dollars that we would be out of the service before the first of July, so that is a pretty good sign that we will be discharged before fall I guess. I will have to close now for I am in a hurry.

Write to me just as quick as you get this for I want to know weather you receive this Beautiful picture, so no more your ever true Brother,
John

John E. Mattoon
21st New York Cavalry Company
Washington DC

And the star spangled Banner will very long wave over the land of the <u>free</u>

This postscript is striking in that John Mattoon recognized the core national value of "liberty" and yet proceeded in the letter to heavily underline in pencil the word "free". What did "freedom" mean to John? Certainly his newfound patriotism provided an impetus to continue his service; additionally he had grown to love the Army because of the adventurous climate and the ever-changing vistas. Yet this was *not* the freedom promised in the Emancipation Proclamation: John did not mention emancipation or slaves, even tangentially, in a single letter. Deep feeling for the plight of black slaves was not any part of his vernacular. John's personal understanding of freedom meant the retention of already held rights and perhaps advancement from the lot of a poor white farm laborer.

Charley Mattoon was one hundred percent correct in his observation about John: "a peacefull home as no charm for me". John the patriotic adventurer for the first time came right out and said it: "I like to be where there is something a going on." His talk of reenlistment with the war already over is indicative of his commitment to the life of a soldier.

Occasionally John's letters elicit a smile or even a laugh. The Shakers were so named for the peculiar ecstatic motion they exhibited while worshipping to rid themselves of evil. John must have known of them first hand since the religion was founded in America in 1774 near Albany, New York and the Mount Lebanon Shaker Society in New Lebanon, New York was the largest Shaker community in the United States. New Lebanon was only a few miles north of John's home in Canaan, New York. His "to lo lodel lodel lo" song must have been taken from their services. For John to say that he loved being a solder as much as Shakers loved their religion seems a significant testament of commitment to his new career. Finally he had found something that he could sink his heart into and in doing well at it, earn some respect.

Maj. Boutelle, who was currently in command of the regiment with Lt. Col. Fitz Simmons on thirty days sick leave, was certainly not in the minority in his assumption that the 21st would be discharged along with most other units of the Union Army. His assumption unfortunately proved wrong; possibly costing him his $1,000 in the process.

A week later, on May 16, John Mattoon indicated to Annie that he was likely staying on as his regiment would probably be kept in service. But he also mentioned that he would need summer employment from Charlotte's husband Horace Bristol, as John still believed he would get a furlough.

Camp At Falls Church Va
May 16th 1865

Dear Sister
Your kind and welcome letter was received this evening and it found me as usual well and enjoying myself. I was sorry to hear that you were not well and that you were a-going to leave Falls Village [Connecticut] for I think that you liked it there first rate, but I suppose that Lotty needs you now very bad for 2 little Babies[5] is rather too much for one woman to take care of so you must go and help her take car of the Baby for I expect to be home by next winter to see it. There is no sign of our being discharged yet awhile they say that they are a gong to keep a good deal of Cavalry so I suppose we will have to stay a while yet. There is no news to write about any more that what I have written. John Hen is well and sends his Love. Most all of the Company is drunk tonight and some are fighting and some are Blowing and another such a noise you never heard I can hardly hear myself think so you must excuse this short letter. Believe me to be you ever true Brother,
John

P. Kiss the new Born Babe [Jenny May Stone] for me and give my Love to Lotty and Horace. So no more it is getting quite late and I guess I shall have to write to Falls Village yet to night to tell Horace to get ready to have me help him through haying this summer. Tell Lotty to write and all the rest of the folks,

J E Mattoon

That regimental discipline had deteriorated to the extent that "most all of the Company is drunk tonight and some are fighting" is not surprising. As a practical matter, the war was over and senior officers were leaving in droves. The officers that were left required only light duty in camp and there were very few diversions for restless soldiers. Many historians have reported that hell-raising behavior ran high in the immediate aftermath of the Civil War. Additionally, in the absence of anything else to do, there was also a great deal of fighting between the rival Eastern and Western Union Armies.[6]

The two biographers of the 21st New York Cavalry differ on whether the regiment participated in the Grand Review that took place in Washington on May 23 and 24. Thomas Reed stated that there were no newspaper accounts of the Griswold Lights' participation, while John Bonnell confidently wrote "Many of the officers took pride in their units and wanted the men to look good; some remained awake most of the night to see that the men were as well groomed as possible for the parade."[7]

John Mattoon wrote to Annie on the ninth of May: "We are going to have a grand review on the 15th all the Armies and most of the army of the Potomac are Camped around Washington and we expect a part of Gen Shermans Army here every day . . . "[8] John got the date and venue wrong and did not write that the regiment actually participated. However it seems likely that they in fact did, because they moved camp across Washington to Bladensburg, Maryland on the evening of the twenty-third.[9]

The euphoria of the Grand Review was soon followed by a return to camp life and the realization that although a number of the one hundred forty eight one-year men (who enlisted as replacements in 1864) as well as selected others were to be mustered out, most would still be required to stay on, although no one knew for how long. According to Reed, "One hundred thirty two one year enlisted men were mustered out and sent home early in June 1865."[10]

By early June, the 21st was in a new camp at Alexandria, Virginia at Cloud's Mill awaiting orders. "While at Cloud's Mill, another one hundred men were mustered out at the beginning of June; eight men were discharged from hospitals; three more men deserted and one man received a dishonorable discharge." Among those discharged from hospitals was Canaan, New York native George "Smoke" Barnes, wounded in the hip at White Post six months earlier.[11] In all, 371 men of the 21st New York Cavalry were subsequently granted early discharge at the end of hostilities, long before their enlistment ended.[12]

II.   The State of the Post-War Union

Washington, led by Republicans in the White House and Congress was scrambling to come up with plans for what would become a policy toward the South called Reconstruction, as well as for the protection of American citizens and economic expansion in the West. Additionally, the heavily armed Mormons in Utah needed to be watched, and federal arsenals and seacoast fortifications needed to be garrisoned.[13] All of this required at least some retention of the volunteer Army until the professional Army could be reconstituted.

The Civil War had been for the North "a time of unprecedented prosperity" with railroads booming, Chicago becoming the Midwest's commercial center on the basis of meat packing, New England's woolen mills flourishing, and agriculture of all types benefiting.[14] The Republicans had created a central banking system to deal with the unprecedented economic expansion as well as the enormous war debt. "At war's end the federal bureaucracy, with 53,000 employees...was the largest employer in the nation" providing "both a vast new patronage machine for the Republican Party and a broad constituency committed to maintaining the integrity of the national state."[15] This policy of protection, unification, and expansion of the larger society would have a direct impact on many veteran units, including the Griswold Lights. During the war there had been no hesitation to use federal troops to put down disruptive strikes, as witnessed by the New York Draft Riots of 1863. Now it appeared that the shrunken postwar military would be assigned the missions of consolidating and expanding the Union that had emerged from the conflict. Cavalry troops were desperately needed to pursue these dual goals.

The military was soon to be dramatically downsized, decentralized and scattered in relatively small posts throughout the country. Congress was now reluctant in the extreme to spend money on a standing Army and nowhere was this more of a problem than in the rapidly expanding Western settlements, where small garrisons faced much larger Indian forces.

III.   Happenings out West

During the Civil War, white immigration into the ancestral lands of the plains Indians had never ceased, and the Indians were growing increasingly disposed to resist threats to their way of life. Liberal land policies instituted by the government included the Homestead Law, signed by Lincoln in 1862, which allowed settlers up to 160 acres of land without cash payment.[16] Just before the War, in the winter and spring of 1859, the discovery of gold near Denver City (erroneously called the Pike's Peak Gold Rush after a recognizable landmark sixty miles to the south) in Colorado Territory set off a massive influx of would-be prospectors into that region. Approximately one hundred thousand people flooded into the Territory, becoming the founders of Denver City, and other outposts of "civilization".[17] But by 1862, census figures showed that number dwindling to only 25,329 in the Territory and 2,603 in Denver itself.[18] Whatever the initial illusions of the lackluster gold rush, Denver remained a vibrant boom town.

These new arrivals were alternately scared, repulsed and fascinated by the American Indians that lived among them. It was a time of relative peace, with few outright attacks but many instances of stolen horses and strained relations. Few if any white men deviated from the general feeling that the indigenous peoples "were dirty, thieving, shiftless and lazy."[19] The new citizens of the Territory discovered they could count on little Federal protection as long as the fighting continued back east. The Cheyenne Indians under Black Kettle, who was known as a "Peace Chief", made war only against the hated Ute tribe as they had always done, not against the whites.[20] Nonetheless, volunteer soldiers and almost all of the citizens on the Colorado Platte were inclined to take a belligerent approach toward the Indians rather than to negotiate with them. This "on the ground" mentality contradicted the policies of forced relocation to reservations and treaty negotiation that the federal government sought to pursue.

Ironically, the government's policy of pursuing westward expansion as well as an unenforceable appeasement strategy brought matters to a head. Both settlers and Indians routinely broke elements of treaty agreements with impunity. The Eastern perception of the noble savage who could be dealt with and trusted (after having been uprooted and driven onto a reservation) was not quite accurate and neither was the settler's image of American Indians as bloodthirsty fiends. Continued white migration into the traditional hunting grounds of the Indians and the friction that it caused would bring matters to a head.

The pivotal historical event in the developing conflict between Native Americans and white settlers on the Colorado Platte was the Sand Creek Massacre. On November 29, 1864, Col. John M. Chivington led his newly formed 3rd Colorado Volunteer Regiment to an encampment of Cheyenne and Arapahoe Indians led by Chief Black Kettle near a bend of Sand Creek. This regiment was no more than a vigilante squad that had the blessing of Colorado Territory. It was formed for one hundred days of service, and its sole purpose was to fight Indians. "Based upon evidence drawn from both military and Congressional hearings, the encounter was described as a merciless slaughter of men, women and children of proven friendly demeanor, who believed they were under the protection of the Colorado authorities."[21] This precipitate event was the result of a policy formulated by Colorado Territorial Governor John Evans, who arrived in 1862 and immediately recognized that the indigenous Indians stood in the way of Colorado Territory's progress toward statehood by slowing pioneer immigration and disrupting communications, not to mention his own occupancy of a newly minted Senate seat in Washington.

The reservation set aside for the Cheyenne and Arapahoe was on poor land and the disgruntled Indians could not be kept within its confines with the meager forces Evans had available. Although there were a few notable instances of Indian depredations in this period, (mostly cattle theft) Evans became convinced through information from traders and Indian agents that the Cheyenne and Arapaho along with elements of the Sioux were planning an uprising for the spring of 1864.[22] As early as November, 1863, Robert North, who lived among the Cheyenne reported to Evans "that the Comanches, Apaches, Kiowas, the northern band of Arapahoes, and all of the Cheyennes, with the Sioux, had pledged one another to go to war with the whites as soon as they could procure ammunition in the spring."[23] By all accounts, Governor Evans accepted the statement at face value and immediately prepared to meet this perceived threat.

The *Rocky Mountain News* in Denver City, Colorado Territory published damning evidence (after the fact) that Evans was not interested in making peace. Months earlier at Camp Weld near Denver City, Black Kettle along with other chiefs were brought in by Maj. John E. Wynkoop to meet with Evans. Black Kettle said "We have come with our eyes shut, following [Maj. Wynkoop's] handful of men, like coming through the fire. All we ask is to have peace with the whites. We want to hold you by the hand. You are our father."[24] Evans responded by saying: "So far as making a treaty now is concerned, we are in no condition to do it. Your young men are on the war path. My soldiers are preparing for the fight. You, so far have had the advantage; but the time is near at hand when the plains will swarm with United States soldiers."[25]

"The Commissioner of Indian Affairs was displeased with Evans's performance at Camp Weld. On October 15, he wrote that it was the governor's duty 'to hold yourself in readiness to encourage and receive the first intimations of a desire on the part of the Indians for a permanent peace'".[26] Washington was correct in assuming that both Evans and Chivington had done nothing to encourage peace. Yet to the Cheyenne, it looked like they had indeed agreed to bury the hatchet.

The Indians returned to the Fort Lyon area, and "as winter neared the raids slowed and stopped as expected; Indians traditionally rested during the cold months."[27] The motley warriors of the 3rd Colorado Cavalry were out in the field under Col. Chivington. These men in no way resembled the United States Army. They were territorial militia with a very personal axe to grind. They were literally picked off the street by Chivington and his officers for one hundred days of fighting Indians. The whole truth about the Sand Creek Massacre will never be known, as some of those who testified about it to the Senate's Joint Committee on the Conduct of the War must have been lying. According to Smith "The Third and the Coloradans it represented, was determined to have its hour of vengeance."[28] And Coloradans were determined to pursue the Indian menace no matter how many Congressional inquiries were set against them, and in spite of federal assurances of protection for the Indians. There was a wide gap between President Andrew Johnson's ideas of placing Indians on reservations "far away from our highways and encroaching white settlements" and aiding in their "moral and intellectual improvement", and the attitude out West.[29] This was the situation that would soon confront the men of the 21st New York Cavalry when they were dispatched to join the fray in Colorado.

IV.   Desertion or Duty – Back in Washington

The cessation of hostilities in the Civil War brought on a large wave of desertions throughout both armies, irrespective of unit or geography. In their minds, soldiers had no reason to stay with their regiments other than to wait for an honorable discharge. The figures for desertion in the Civil War are notoriously inconsistent. An historian analyzing the "statistics" for rates of desertion in the period must take into account the individual inclinations of company commanders to accept any and all excuses for an absent soldier *other* than desertion, which reflected poorly upon their command. Such excuses as "absent, sick at muster out" leading to the simple "medical discharge" were common subterfuges to hide desertion.

Ella Lonn, in what is still the only lengthy discussion on the matter; *Desertion During the Civil War* (1928) concluded that the motives for desertion were similar for both North and South in the Civil War in that they were predominantly personal and emotional rather than representing any erosion in broadly held ideological views. There is also evidence to suggest that poorly led regiments had higher instances of desertion. This was also true of some units that experienced more combat and suffered more battle losses than others. As previously mentioned, certain upward spikes in desertion follow a pattern; men who should never have been soldiers or who were habitual bounty jumpers were filtered out in the first month or two. Desertions continued during the conflict but at a much decreased level for a variety of generally personal reasons although there is reason to believe that some veteran units lost men before going into battle. The next major upswing in desertions occurred when the end of the war was assured.

Desertions accelerated in the case of the 21st New York Cavalry as the remaining men in the Regiment were told sometime during the week after the Grand Review that they would not be mustered out. These men were on the verge of finally returning to their homes and families and a continuation of their postwar lives. They viscerally knew that they were no longer needed to fight the good fight for the preservation of the Union, and that if they were kept in service they would be posted either down south to enforce the infant policy of Reconstruction or out west to fight Indians. Neither of those scenarios held much interest for a Civil War veteran yearning to go home.

In the Union Army as a whole, the number of deserters per month from 1863 to 1865 averaged 5,500 with 10,692 deserting (or, at least, being reported as having deserted) in October 1864.[30] For all troops North and South, the Provost Marshal General James Fry reported 278,644 desertions, but added: "This number is much too large. Many of those reported as deserters are not so in reality, but are men who became unavoidably absent from their commands by falling sick on the march, being injured in action without the knowledge of their officers, and reported 'missing, and subsequently deserted', and by intentionally or unintentionally overstaying their furloughs, &c., &c." His final estimation was that about 201,000 actually deserted.[31] Ella Lonn concluded that during the whole course of the War one out of every seven men deserted from the Union Army.[32] Historical Data Systems of Duxbury, Massachusetts which publishes the online data site *Civil War Data* states that there were a total of 4,324,196 soldiers that fought for both the North and South. However this number is artificially high. Those rolls include huge numbers of men that enlisted but never served, many enlisting multiple times. Of that population, they describe 215,963 as disabled, 185,866 deserted, and 227,015 were marked as discharged.[33] It is unlikely that a firm count for "desertion" will ever be extrapolated from that data as regiments North and South wished to cover up that damning number as much as possible and hide it in other statistical columns.

V.   The 21st at War's End

1,752 officers and men served in the 21st New York Cavalry from June 1863 to September 1866. This seems a reasonable estimate based upon all of the available data. It must be noted that approximately two hundred and fifty men were carried on recruiting rolls but not mustered in, or deserted within the first sixty days.[34] The vast majority were three-year enlistees. Only 148 replacements enlisted late in 1864 for one year of service.[35] There were seventeen regimental officers and twelve company officers for each of the original twelve companies, making 161 officers commanding the 1340 enlisted men who actually served.

On May 30, 1865 the remaining thirty one-year men were mustered out after the May twenty-third Grand Review Parade. The rest of the 21st, approximately 580 men, were left wondering why they were still in uniform.[36] They had no idea how unlucky they actually were.

Regimental biographer Thomas Reed reported that "On June 3, 1865, the War Department directed General Auger to send two cavalry brigades . . . to the Army of the Tennessee."[37] On June 10 those orders were amended to put General Tibbits in charge of a brigade to join Maj. Gen. John Pope's Dept. of the Mississippi.[38] The new brigade was to be formed from the 21st New York Cavalry, the 14th Pennsylvania and the 6th West Virginia. Colonel Fitz Simmons returned from sick leave with orders that they were to be transferred to "Indian Country." No other information was forthcoming. The three-year enlistees who had signed up in late 1863 still had more than a year left to serve. Although many cavalry units were summarily disbanded at the time, the 21st was unlucky in being picked for further duty. It is certainly likely that Brevet General Will Tibbits, who wanted to continue his Army career, placed himself in a more politically secure position by volunteering his veteran cavalry.

That spring, John's father and mother had moved down the road from Canaan to Falls Village, Connecticut:

Alexandria Va June 12th 1865

Dear Sister,

Your Letter was received a good while ago and have neglected to answer it so long on account of having no postage stamps. Well Ann I guess I shan't see Canaan this summer. Very bad for me. We are now under marching orders to go to St Louis, Missuria. We expected to break Camp this morning but did not, we may go away today and then maybe we will not Leave for a week to come. I don't care how soon we leave here for I don't like it here there is nothing a-going on at all. Well Annie when did you hear from home last? I have not heard from there since you left – yes I did! I had one letter from Len [Lenny

Mattoon] a few days ago but I have had none from Falls Village yet and have given up thinking about getting one. How does Lot's Baby get along? I hope it is well, [but an] awful name Lot has given it: Laura Crocket. O tell her not to name it Laura any way for all the darndest names that ever I heard that is the worst of any tell her to name it Clary or Helen or Margaret or Charlotte or Clandy or Francis or Julia or Sarah or any thing but that awful name Laura. Lord what ever possessed her to think of calling it that? Tell her if she names her young one that I will inlist in the regulars for 5 years or else go to sea or else commit suicide. That's all. Give my love to Horace and to Lot, so if she won't name her Babe Laura tell her to name it any thing else and it will suit me. I don't care what it is if it is polliformagy. Well Annie here is 23 cheers for Missura any way! Hurah Hurah Hurah and with that I will close rite away. Write soon and direct as usual.

J E Mattoon

Poor Charlotte. John's ranting about the Bristol's second child, who is listed in the *Mattoon Family Genealogy* as "Lula" (although subsequent investigation has revealed that she was actually named "Laura Margaret" and was born on May 10, 1865) is either remarkably petulant or a remarkable example of dry humor. Bell Wiley in *The Life of Billy Yank* noted that "Billy Yank was an inveterate tease and prankster"[39] and it would seem that John Mattoon was not above such antics. Of greater interest is John's insistence that they were being sent to St. Louis, Missouri, and his impatience to get away. His "23 cheers for Missura" seems almost more heartfelt than his sorrow at not getting a furlough to see Canaan and his family again. The professional soldier and the restless farm boy still wanted action.

The desertions of the enlisted men of the 21st New York Cavalry were immediate and heavy. The men started leaving in Virginia almost immediately after the announcement that the regiment would continue on. It appeared that only a core group of motivated men would be left to prosecute whatever that mission might be.

Notes

1. Personal remembrances of loved ones (living or dead) using their hair made into or kept within jewelry pieces was a common practice in Victorian America.
2. Balls Cross Roads is not mentioned in the *OR*. Some of Mosby's men were in the vicinity of Berryville, Virginia on April 8th where Tibbits and his officers were housed. Eight men were standing as pickets as the rebels crept up to ambush them. Two privates were killed; Andrew McCartney of F Company and William A. Manderville of A Company. Three were wounded and three taken prisoner. They may have been the last combat deaths in the Shenandoah Valley. See Reed, 236; Bonnell, 178–9
3. Ibid.

4.   John E. Mattoon to Annie Mattoon Stone, *Mattoon Letters*, (April 28, 1865)
5.   Charlotte by now had borne Sarah and her second daughter Laura.
6.   Bonnell, 185
7.   Ibid., 183
8.   John E. Mattoon to Annie Mattoon Stone, *Mattoon Letters*, (May 9, 1865)
9.   Bonnell, 183
10.   Reed, 237; See also Bonnell, 181
11.   Bonnell, 185; Reed, 288
12.   Ibid., 300
13.   Robert Allen Wooster. *The Military and United States Indian Policy; 1865–1903*. (New Haven: Yale University Press, 1988), 14–15
14.   Eric Foner, *Reconstruction: America's Unfinished Revolution 1863–1877*. (New York: Harper & Row 1988; Reprint HarperCollins, Perennial Classics, 2002), 18–19
15.   Ibid., 23
16.   Reed, 245
17.   Duane A. Smith. *The Birth of Colorado, a Civil War Perspective*. (Norman, OK: Univ. of Oklahoma Press, 1989), 6
18.   Ibid., 14
19.   Duane Schultz. *Month of the Freezing Moon: The Sand Creek Massacre, November, 1864*. (New York: St. Martin's Press, 1990), 43
20.   Schultz, 51
21.   David Sivaldi, *Sand Creek and the Rhetoric of Extermination: a Case Study in Indian-White Relations*. (Boston: University Press of America, 1989), 5
22.   Shultz, 66
23.   George Bird Grinnell. *The Fighting Cheyenne*. (Norman: University of Oklahoma Press, 1915), 135
24.   *Rocky Mountain News*, (September 13, 1865), 2 Col. 1
25.   Ibid., 3 Col. 2
26.   Schultz, 114
27.   Smith, 214
28.   Ibid., 218
29.   Wooster, 44
30.   Lonn, 151–2
31.   Ibid., 89, 230
32.   Ibid., 226
33.   Data Set, *Civil War Database*, online at: http://www.civilwardata.com /active/hdsquery.dll?RegimentDynamics?ALL&all&all&P&2; Accessed July 12, 2006.
34.   Reed, 300
35.   Ibid., 44
36.   This number is my approximation using information from Reed, Bonnell, and the *Civil War Database*.
37.   Reed, 237
38.   Ibid.
39.   Wiley, 171

CHAPTER FIVE

I.   On the Road

On June 13, 1865 the 21st New York Cavalry was ordered onto a Baltimore & Ohio train headed for Parkersburg, West Virginia.[1] The 3rd West Virginia Cavalry was to embark at the same time. Many of the 3rd were drunk and disorderly and started taunting the 21st as "cowards" and "boots."[2] The 3rd West Virginia was under the command of General George A. Custer and wore the same red flannel necktie that he did, earning them the name "red necks." They also appropriated some of the proud and egotistical swagger of Custer, a fearless cavalry officer and a darling of the media. Equally fearless and much less well known, with perhaps a bit of a chip on their shoulders, the boys of the 21st would take no abuse. "Someone in the Griswold Lights lost his temper and decked one of the Virginians."[3] A riot ensued in which wild shots were fired by the 3rd West Virginia, doing no reported harm. Since the 21st New York had no ammunition, they used their sabers. The fighting was finally stopped when officers of both commands brought it under control.[4] Records indicate there were no deaths but there must have been many injuries. Surprisingly John Mattoon did not write home about this incident, or perhaps the letter has been lost. However a letter dated May 30, 1906 was written to John E. and Anna Haight Mattoon from Stephen H. Draper, late 2nd Lieutenant in Company K of the 21st who had been mustered out on May 15, 1865 due to injury.[5] The letter was certainly sent in remembrance of the fortieth anniversary of the end of the 21st's service. Draper wrote of the 308 men "lost during its service" and the "60 battles and skirmishes, the list being too long to enumerate." To those gallant and historic acts Draper added: "their affray with Custer's Red Neckties at Washington D.C."[6] Forty years after the fact, the impression the riot left in the mind of Lt. Draper of the 21st remained vivid. In recalling it in his letter, Draper was undoubtedly speaking of an event still thought of with great satisfaction and amusement by the veterans of the Griswold Lights.

Now on board the slow and overcrowded train heading in a westerly direction, the men were very curious as to their ultimate destination and were in a generally unruly and wholly unmanageable state. A contingent of the cavalrymen took it upon themselves to terrorize the local populace when the train stopped at various stations. Upon arrival in Sandy Hook, Maryland some of the 21st "overwhelmed local merchants in their desire to acquire goods. In the confusion created by the press of the soldiers, the lawbreakers concealed in the crowd commenced robbing the merchants of liquor, watches, clothing and other articles." As well, "The officers apparently made no attempt to restrain the men."[7] The looting began again in Martinsburg and resumed at Station No. 12 in West Virginia. The train did not stop again until Cumberland, where word had spread by telegraph of the depredations caused by the 21st. The train was met by the provost marshal and surrounded by his men, who promptly placed the whole command under arrest.[8] Captain Peter Hogeboom, the officer in charge of the train, and five other officers were immediately cashiered, never receiving a court martial, although by Presidential Decree that judgment was later changed to honorable discharge.[9] With the men of the 21st still under arrest, the train was allowed to go to Parkersburg, where seven men deserted, doubtless to escape punishment as ringleaders. The remaining Griswold Lights were released on June 20 (with their pay garnished until October to compensate merchants for their losses) to continue their trip to St. Louis.[10] They were loaded onto two boats, the *Nora* and the *Tyrone* for the river trip, arriving in East St. Louis on June 23.[11]

In the aftermath of the reprehensible behavior on the first leg of the trip, and certainly to avoid punishment, one of the first things that many men of the 21st did when disembarking at the port of St. Louis was to desert. In fact, there was substantial and increasing ill will among elements of the regiment who had become certain that they were to be mustered out in St. Louis. Instead they found they were to be part of a brigade consisting of the 14th Pennsylvania, 3rd Massachusetts and 6th West Virginia Cavalry, headed to Colorado Territory.[12] The 21st was in St. Louis only about five days from June 23 to June 28 before moving out, but in that time twenty five men deserted.[13] Men who would charge into Confederate cannons were now giving evidence of their unwillingness to accept the uncertainty and undoubted hardship of service on the Great Plains of America. The men surely thought that it the regular Army's business to fight the American Indian, and not veteran volunteers. The morale problem was severely weakening the regiment. The enlisted men were not the only ones leaving: their commander Lt. Col. Fitz Simmons was struck down with typhoid fever on the trip to St. Louis and had to return home to New York State on sick leave.[14]

On or around the Fourth of July, 1865, after a train ride of three hundred and nine miles due west, the 21st found themselves at the large, hot, and dusty outpost of Fort Leavenworth, Kansas. The Command was split in two, with Major Otis and Major Boutelle taking equally sized detachments across the plains. The large quartermaster depot was able to outfit the regiment quickly, although some men had to wait for mounts due to an endemic shortage of horses.[15] They were supposed to have been a part of a major 1865 campaign to protect citizens and assets as well as punish the hostile tribes of Indians on the Great Plains for their real or perceived transgressions. Brig. Gen. Patrick Connor, an Irishman and experienced Indian fighter, was in charge of this "Powder River" expedition, which left Denver in early July. This effort to bring the Cheyenne, Sioux and Arapaho under control was regarded as a failure, mostly due to the fact that there was very little actual contact with hostile elements.[16] Another major reason for the lack of success according to an historian of the campaign "was the [poor] attitude of the [volunteer] troops and their officers."[17] General Grenville Mellon Dodge, then commander of the Department of the Missouri, ended up receiving only half the men he requested, and most of them arrived with no interest in fighting.

At least one of the Griswold Lights kept his cantankerous fighting spirit, although it must have been highly tested as John Mattoon wrote to his sister Annie about his cousin John Henry Mattoon, his last remaining friend, cousin, and confidante from Canaan:

Camp Near Leavenworth City
Kansas July 8th 1865

Dear Sister,

I thought that I would write you a few lines to night to let you know that I am still alive and well but a good ways from home. Well Annie, John Hen has deserted so I am the only one left in the 21st NY Cav. From Canaan but I never shall desert as long as there is one man left in the Regt. Well Annie they say that we have to cross the plains and go to Santy Fee New Mexico, so I shall have to stay my time out in the service but such I can stand. If I can't I don't know who can. I suppose Charley Mattoon has got home before this time I hope so any way. It is getting so dark that I can't see to write any more so good night and pleasant dreams I will finish in the morning. J E Mattoon

Sunday Morning July 9th

Well Annie I will finish my letter now when we cross the plains they say we will have to go 3 days without water and fight Indians and the devil only knows what else. So they try to make us think that we will never get across but men have gone across before so it is a pity – if we can do it. I shall have to close now give my love to Lot and Horace and Kiss the Babies for their uncle John.

John E Mattoon

Direct Washington DC

John would never have used the word desertion in a letter home (potentially branding his cousin for life in his home town) if he did not have firsthand information he believed truthful. What finally drove John Henry Mattoon to desert is not known, but the prospect of the continuing hardships of campaigning for at least another year in hostile territory must have weighed heavily on his mind. Additionally, unlike John E., John Hen had a young wife at home. At the regimental level desertion was by now so widespread that it carried less of a stigma in the ranks. It certainly had come down to who was hard enough to take the continued punishment of service. John Mattoon's personal opinion on the matter was quite clear. His patriotism and lust for adventure were still as strong as ever: "I never shall desert as long as there is one man left in the Regt." But he did not castigate his cousin for his act. Not surprisingly the staff officers of the 21st recorded the event as a "discharge" dated June 23.

In *The Vacant Chair* (1993), social historian Reid Mitchell put forward the thesis that "small-unit cohesion" turned Army companies into surrogate families for soldiers. Years of living and fighting together forged close bonds of personal loyalty and interdependence: "Leaving the army meant leaving behind men with whom one had served, suffered, and risked one's life. The affections of this substitute family competed with the claims of the family a soldier had left at home."[18] It must have been terribly hard on John to lose his cousin, and the decision to desert must have been a difficult and wrenching one for John Henry Mattoon as well.

As for John's reference to a possible posting to Santa Fe, New Mexico, there is no recorded information that the 21st might have been headed there. The deceptive warnings gleaned from other soldiers at Fort Leavenworth regarding crossing the Plains, such as having to go "3 days without water and fight Indians" could indicate some real apprehension on John's part, but also seem a bit of a tall tale meant to wryly cultivate John's "hard man" image for Annie and the family back home, and perhaps for the benefit of the ladies such as Miss Hobert or the mysterious "EE."

II.   Tibbits' Waterloo

The Griswold Lights were encamped at Leavenworth with the three other regiments in their brigade. The 6th West Virginia proved to be the most volatile in the mix. They had seen many battles, but orders to march to Salt Lake City nine hundred miles away pushed them over the edge.[19] When commanded to move out for Fort Kearney, Nebraska on the morning of July 15, the majority of the 6th stayed in their tents. Informed of the mutiny by their indecisive commander, Colonel Fleming, General Will Tibbits stormed out of headquarters and rounded up the 21st New York Cavalry and a battery of howitzers and headed for the encampment of the 6th West Virginia.

Accounts vary, with some saying that Tibbits ordered his men to open fire and the men refusing to do so, others not mentioning any such order. But in the face of angry armed men who refused to follow orders, "Tibbits ordered the men [of the 6th] to turn in their Spencer rifles and horse furniture, and surprisingly the men did so without resistance." Three ringleaders were imprisoned and later sentenced to life imprisonment at hard labor.[20]

Brig. Gen. Christopher Stolbrand was senior officer at the time at Fort Leavenworth. Technically Tibbits' junior, he nonetheless ordered him arrested on the afternoon of July 15 upon the supposition that Tibbits proposed to fire on "his" troops. Stolbrand had no way to actually confine Tibbits at post without risking a full scale riot, as Tibbits had a full brigade under his command. Tibbits immediately returned to St. Louis and put the matter before Gen. Dodge, "who gave a verbal order releasing him from arrest and reinstating him to command."[21] However, because the order was not written, a fierce struggle for control between the two generals meant that it took another two weeks to finally get the 21st on the road again. In the aftermath of this altercation, over a month passed with Tibbits and the recently returned Col. Fitz Simmons preparing the defense. For unknown reasons no court martial was ever convened. However by the time Tibbits reached Fort Kearney in early September, he learned that the 21st New York Cavalry Regiment was to be consolidated into a battalion of seven companies, leaving him a "surplus" general officer with a command too small for his rank. As such, he was ordered back to Troy, New York. Arriving there in October, he promptly left the service.[22]

The desertion rate at Fort Leavenworth remained high with six men soon listed as missing, and in the wake of the 6th West Virginia mutiny, approximately 120 men were discharged or mustered out of the 21st New York Cavalry, likely for refusing to join in the trek to Fort Kearney, for general insubordination or for "illness". Thus a consolidation order was handed down which made the regiment into a battalion of only around 420 men in total. John Mattoon's Company L, in which he had been placed for his entire service up to that point, was no more. He was moved to Company F on September ninth.

The 21st had been on a long, dusty and hot road since late July. General Dodge in St. Louis feared that if he did not get all of his new troops moving at once he risked losing most of them to desertion. He knew that the remnants of the 6th West Virginia "along with the 21st New York, were already on the road west, but were moving 'slower than ox teams.'"[23] He also knew quite well and to his peril that the volunteers he had been given were "dissatisfied, mutinous and inefficient" and just wanted to go home.[24]

There was no question that when they could, the 21st dragged their feet, perhaps with the complicity of their junior officers. The General officers had other ideas however, and when Otis' detachment finally arrived at Fort Kearney on August 10, they were immediately hurried back onto the trail with only four days rest. They moved onward to duty at newly built Fort Collins, Colorado to

guard the telegraph and Overland Stage route.[25] The men followed the old
Oregon Trail west along the Platte River and then more northerly to Julesburg,
Colorado, a distance of one hundred eighty miles. With new supplies and
guides, the 21st New York marched again and finally made the almost one
thousand mile trek from St. Louis to Fort Collins in early September, having
taken seventy days for an average of a little over fourteen miles a day.[26] During
this lengthy period en route, fifty nine desertions took place, or over thirteen
percent of the force that left the Shenandoah Valley, dramatically depleting a
unit that already had lost many men through a variety of "discharges", illness or
other happenstance. The 21st now comprised just over four hundred officers
and men.[27]

III.   Fort Collins

Tiny and new, Fort Collins had already been the scene of serious incidents of
disobedience. One of the regiments that the 21st was sent to relieve, the 11th
Kansas Cavalry, had mutinied in late July, saying their enlistments had expired.
The officers of the regiment disputed this assertion and the mutiny was put
down by other units that were raced to the scene, but "several companies of the
regiment continued to be insubordinate and rebellious."[28] Only the timely arrival
of the soon to be mustered out 1st, 6th, and 7th Michigan Cavalry Regiments
kept them in line for a time, until it was recognized that they were essentially
useless and were finally disbanded and allowed to go back to Kansas in
August.[29]

Fort Collins was a small post that had been just been established on the
banks of the Cache la Poudre River in 1863. "In the spring of 1864, Lieutenant
Colonel W.O. Collins, commander at Fort Laramie, Wyoming, sent two
companies from the 11th Ohio Volunteer Cavalry under the command of Captain
William H. Evans to staff the post."[30] It was called Camp Collins in honor of the
locally popular Colonel Collins. When its initial site was deemed inappropriate,
the post was moved to a new site in August of 1864. This site became the future
location of the modern city of Fort Collins, Colorado.

Buildings on the post included company quarters, a kitchen, a guardhouse,
company stables, a hospital, an orderly room, officers' quarters, laundresses'
quarters, and a sutler's store.[31] It did not have an encircling stockade fence, as
the oxbow in the river was thought to act as at least three sides of an effective
defense.

While the 21st had been at war and then marching toward Colorado, the
seeds that the Sand Creek Massacre had sown were beginning to flower. By
early spring of 1865, Fort Rankin and Julesburg, Colorado had suffered Indian
attacks. Many of the Overland Trail stations between Denver and the Platte to
the north were burned out. Chivington's successor, Col. Thomas Moonlight, was
forced to proclaim martial law in Colorado Territory.[32] "Ranches and coach

stations lay in smoking ruins, some fifty whites were killed and others captured, six hundred tons of government hay burned, and uncounted quantities of food and supplies stolen." Denver City "was threatened with famine as food supplies dwindled."[33] Governor Evans was at the time in Washington, defending himself before Congressional Hearings on the Sand Creek Massacre. Eventually the appalling complicity of Evans and Chivington regarding Sand Creek became public knowledge and Secretary of State William H. Seward sent President Johnson's request for Evans' resignation on July 18, 1865. In the interim, acting Governor Samuel Elbert wrote Washington of the Denver area's serious problems, concluding: "The general government must help us or give up the territory to the Indians."[34] The nationally disgraced but locally revered 3rd Colorado Cavalry had been mustered out, and in the wake of the official enquiry into Sand Creek, it was proving difficult to recruit local men who, even though they were eager to protect their own homes, balked at having to deal with a distant Washington "which so delights in abusing and vilifying the soldiers who fought the battle of Sand Creek."[35]

Continued frenzied entreaties for help from Denver and other communities were what eventually led the central Army command in St. Louis to send out the 21st New York and many other reluctant regiments to reinforce the string of forts in the region. This was not done without trepidation however. The Army knew that Congress was desperate to keep the military budget down, and that there was a well-known disconnect between the realities Western settlers knew and lived with and the official position taken by the federal government and administration in Washington. Gen. William Tecumseh Sherman noted that "There are two classes of people, one demanding the utter extinction of the Indians and the other full of love for their conversion to civilization and Christianity. Unfortunately the Army stands in between and gets the cuffs from both sides."[36]

It would be impossible to overstate the resistance to anything resembling appeasement of the Indians among residents of Colorado Territory at this time. Calls for negotiation or any other kind of moderate treatment of the Indians came only from Eastern newspapers, government agents, a few officers of the Army, and recent Eastern transplants. The *Rocky Mountain News* in Denver was not apologetic: "We have been classed among the defenders of Sand Creek. We accept the title, and so long as there is a hostile Indian to kill, we shall be found in favor of the same being done, in any manner that may present itself, the more expeditiously the better."[37]

The *Rocky Mountain News,* the preeminent daily newspaper in Denver at the time, reported in July, "Troops are now being stationed on the Overland Mail road from Denver to the summit of the Rocky Mountains." They also noted the impending arrival of the various regiments sent out from Fort Leavenworth, including the 21st New York: "A regiment of this cavalry is now en route from [Fort] Kearney and will be placed on the telegraph line as soon as it arrives."[38]

According to the newspaper the troops' imperative mission was to protect the movement of people and goods. An example of the Griswold Lights' duties was published in September: "Gov. Evans left [Denver] this morning for Empire, where he goes to distribute the goods to the Utes of Middle Park . . . The wagons loaded with these annuities left for their destinations yesterday morning, under an escort of the Twenty First N.Y. Cavalry."[39]

Fort Collins was still very new and very raw in the fall of 1865. It had only been designated a "Fort" that spring. As Col. Fitz Simmons, the new commander of the 21st, was in Denver convening a court martial, it was left to individual company commanders to oversee the task of guarding the Overland Stage trail and the telegraph lines. Some Companies were moved north that fall to nearby Fort Halleck and remained there to relieve the remainder of the 1st Michigan Cavalry.[40]

The legendary Ben Holladay had purchased the Overland Stage Line in 1862. The line was the most important part of the communications link with the West Coast and points east as well. The Colorado Governor's Office in 1866 reported to Congress that "The overland coaches which leave and arrive here daily have taken in and brought out over 4,000 passengers, and have also brought here $2,400,000 in specie and carried out 26,000 pounds of express freight. Freighting business in this city is seven times greater this year than in 1861 . . . the most experienced freighters think that the trade in 1866 will be nearly *double* that of the past year."[41]

However, periodic Indian attacks could bring the freight and passenger service to a halt. The trail itself was moved a number of times and parallel routes were often used depending on conditions. To a great degree, mail contracts supported the stage line. In 1864, to meet stipulations for a new bid, the U.S. Postal Service required that the line be moved about four miles east of Namaqua to Washburn Station. A few months later, the Overland Trail was moved back to its original location."[42] Depredations to the Line were not limited to attacks by the Native Americans, but were perpetrated by lawless whites and most interestingly by the "protective" soldiers themselves:

A vast amount of damage was done between October, 1864, and December, 1865, by the United States soldiers, who visited stations whenever they felt like it and helped themselves to anything they wanted which happened to be in sight. They indiscriminately took hay, grain, provisions, fuel, etc. At one time they took twenty-nine head of oxen at Fort Kearney, worth $100 a head; and 100 cords of wood at Julesburg, worth fifty dollars a cord. When a receipt was wanted for property taken it was refused. To stop the raids on the stations by the soldiers a military order was procured. Geo. K. Otis, the general superintendent for several years, made a careful estimate of the property taken, which he placed at $30,000. Mr. Carlyle, who for years transported most of the supplies for the stage line, testified that $30,000 was not an overestimate of the damage inflicted by the military on the stage line. David Street also testified that the line was subjected to serious losses in consequence of damage done and property taken by the soldiers. William Reynolds, superintendent of the line from October, 1864, to March, 1866, stated that large quantities of hay, grain and wood were consumed by the military on the stage line, the property of Holladay; also, several houses and stables were used for fuel and other purposes. The losses sustained by Holladay from Indian depredations from 1862 to 1865 were enormous, and ran up into the hundreds of thousands.[43]

Although there were a few unsubstantiated claims from ranchers regarding the conduct of the Griswold Lights, there was never any evidence of harm to the populace caused by the regiment.

Winter came early in the high country. "The detachments of the 21st New York were removed from their guard posts on the stage road for the winter about the first of November and transferred to Fort Collins."[44] The much vaunted 1865 military push against the Indians had come to little more than an increased military presence around settled areas and the protection of most of the Overland Stage route. General John Pope was now in command of the Division of the Missouri and "it was apparent that the 1865 offensives, conducted by units largely made up of volunteers, had not solved the Indian problem. Army columns had encountered only scattered tribes and cost the government over twenty million dollars."[45] Pope and his superior, General Sherman, knew that they had to eventually procure regular cavalry to replace the poor-performing veteran units and the local volunteers if they were to vigorously prosecute any punitive actions against the Indians. In the meantime, if the units on the ground could at least protect citizens and communications, then a new plan could be formulated for 1866 and 1867.

In their initial few weeks of service in "Indian Territory" The Griswold Lights hardly saw an American Indian. In fact the 21st "would take no casualties from hostile action during its stay on the western frontier."[46] The Cheyenne and Sioux did not traditionally make war during the winter, so a few months of calm ensued. This respite allowed the officers of the 21st to start mustering out some of the men who had enlisted earliest. Some one hundred sixteen men were released before the official mustering out of the remainder of the regiment. By the spring of 1866 there would be barely three hundred Griswold Lights left.

Encamped for the winter, it appears that John Mattoon once again had time on his hands to write letters. Back in New York State, John's father William Mattoon had passed away on October 14 at the age of 58.[47] The letter below indicates that mail service was extremely slow and this may account for the very few letters that have survived from this period of John's service to his country.

Camp Collins Colorado Tert.
Dec 18th 1865

Dear Sister,

Your kind and welcome letter was received in due time and the news of Fathers death was not wholy unexpected for I had not had a letter from home in so long that I expected bad news and I had dreamt for two nights running that I see a dead man.   When you write me again I wish you to write all the particulars of his death, what his disease was and how long he was sick and I wish you would tell Charles Haight [Sarah Mattoon's husband, John's former employer, and his future brother in law] to get some tomb stones for him and Mother both and Charge to my account with him.   Tell him to get some nice ones.   I wish I could of been home for a little while before he died for I would have liked to have seen him once more but he has gone and we will all have to follow him some time or other.

Well Annie how are you getting along with Lotties' Babies? I hope they are not cross for it is trouble enough to take care of good babies let alone cross ones but if they take after Lot they are pretty good ones I will warrant you.   I was very glad to hear that John Hen[ry Mattoon] and Charley Mattoon had got out of the army, but I don't know when I will get out or get payed off either.   I have got 12 months pay a-coming to me and 2 installments making in all 232 dollars but the lord only knows when I will get it.   But I hain't got but one more year to serve and then they will have to pay me and discharge me both.   I wrote to Haight the other day and I hope he will answer it for I hain't had a letter from him since I can remember.   I wonder what old Orlando Warriner said to John Hen when he saw him I would like to have seen him and hid some where so they could not see me.   I don't believe I would have had any guts in me for I should of laughed them all out. Tell Horace that Collorado Territory is a Bully place but I can't see it, there are too much Rocky Mountains for me.   I heard a good deal of talk about Pikes Peak when I was there but I never got to see it but I have seen the notorious gold regions and a dreary place it is.   Well, Annie I think that I shall give old Brigham Young a call before I come home for we are now within 150 miles of Salt Lake City.   I would like to go and see what for a place it is. You must give my love to all the folks and reserve a pretty good share for your self please. Answer this rite away for I am anxious to hear from home again. Tell Lot and uncle Horace to write to me and I will answer all the letters I get. Now Annie I will close for I have wrote untill I can hardly see so good bye.

From your ever true Brother,

John E Mattoon

P. Direct to J E Mattoon Company L
21st NY Cavalry Camp Collins Colorado Territory Via
Leavenworth City Kansas

John covered a lot of territory in this letter. The strained nature of his relationship with his father and mother, never terribly close at the best of times, is clearly exhibited by his lukewarm response to his father's death. He didn't mention writing his mother at all only that he wished he could have seen them both one more time. The offer to buy tombstones (on credit) appears to be more of a reflexive response than anything else, as was his closing statement that "we will all have to follow him some time or other". Emotion that does ring true can be sensed in John's happiness in hearing that his cousin and brother had arrived home safely.

It is shocking that John Mattoon had a year's pay due to him. Two-hundred thirty-two dollars was a great deal of money in 1865, and with the newly increased safety along the stage lines, it is amazing that the federal government would not want the rebellious volunteer regiments paid in some timely fashion to reward them for their services. An explanation may lie in the abundance of tantalizing sin available in the frontier towns nearby.

John Mattoon had written about Orlando Wariner from Camp Stow in Halltown, Virginia on Apr 25, 1864. He was a "Canaan boy" too, but the 38-year-old was obviously not liked: "Orlando Wariner turned in his horse saddle and every thing he had and has gone off somewhere, we think he's gone to Frederick City to the General Hospital. He is a mean old skunk any way and we were all glad to get rid of him. We heckterd him a most to death poor fellow . . . "[48] Wariner was listed by New York State as having been "discharged for disability" on April 8, 1865, so he would have been back home by May. It appears that John E. and John H. may have hounded the much older man out of the Army, which would account for John's mirth in contemplating the meeting of his cousin and Wariner.

Evidently John mostly saw little but dusty trails and boredom interspersed with a few periods of hard service. He said very little of the natural wonders of the area. That the "notorious gold regions" were a "dreary place" is certainly likely. A modern-day trip west from Denver on Interstate 70 reveals upon entering the Rockies a host of abandoned holes in the mountainsides with their characteristic tailing piles slung below. The life of a prospector must have been truly "dreary". Finally there are indications that John shared in the mingled fascination and revulsion with which most Americans of his time regarded the secretive, polygamist Mormon society in Utah.

The scouting routine out of the Fort was cold and miserable, but not unduly hazardous. There were very few stagecoaches that could travel in winter weather, but when there were, they were accompanied by a detachment from Camp Collins or another closer post. During a thaw in January, the men even played a game of baseball on the parade ground.[49]

If a pass could be acquired, the only nearby place to go was Denver City. Officially founded in 1858, Denver at that time was a town of about four to five thousand inhabitants, much smaller and more compact than it had been during the earlier gold rush. It had the usual mix of bars, brothels, and amusements of a frontier "city." A public ordinance that required the use of brick for building after a disastrous fire in 1863 and an equally devastating flood in 1864 was dramatically changing the downtown by the winter of 1865–6.

By 1866 Denver had nine billiard halls, two theaters, six restaurants, four wholesale liquor sellers, twenty seven hotels and boarding houses; four tobacconists, and fifteen saloons.[50] These numbers are most likely quite low, as those counted establishments certainly paid a subscription to be in the period pamphlet that lists them, and smaller outfits may not have felt it necessary to be included. The number of houses of ill repute was unsurprisingly not listed, although William Hepworth Dixon, an English visitor, wrote of Denver in 1866: "as you wander about these hot and dirty streets, you seem to be walking in a city of demons. Every fifth house appears to be a bar, a whiskey shop, a lager-beer saloon; every tenth house appears to be either a brothel or a gaming house; very often both in one."[51]

John Mattoon never mentioned Denver in his letters, and it is entirely possible that due to a lack of pay he spent little time there. It was, however, a much sought after watering hole and central meeting place for the many soldiers inhabiting the region of the Central Platte.

Relations with the local populace were quite friendly. The remaining officers of the 21st New York seem to have been universally liked. On January third, 1866, The *Rocky Mountain News* reported that "Col. Fitz Simmons is leaving Denver after duty as President of a general Court-martial for Fort Collins to take command. That is a very important part of Gen. Upton's District and the General has used his usual discrimination in selecting Col. F. to take charge of affairs there. We are sorry to see him leave."[52]

Winter encampment in Colorado was luxurious compared to the ragged conditions the Griswold Lights had experienced in the Shenandoah Valley. There was very light work, plenty of food, no picket duty, and sturdy quarters.[53]

John wrote Annie again on January 17:

Camp Collins
Colorado Territory
Jan 17th 1866

Dear Sister,

Your welcome letter was received this Afternoon and read with pleasure. I was very glad to hear that the folks in Canaan had found a gold mine but I am afraid that it won't amount to much. I think that the California Gold mines would be more profitable that the Canaan mines! I think I shall go and see some of them before I come home anyway. Well Annie, I am serving my last year in the army and when It is out then Ho! for Calif. or some where else. We have not seen any wild Indians in a good while every thing is still here, there is nothing a-going on at all. I have got just as nice a horse as ever stood on 4 legs he is a small sorrel and he can just run every thing in camp. Tell Horace that I wish I was with him tonight – I bet – I would get some Cider and Apples and maybe a chew of fine cut tobacco but it will probably be a long time before I will be with him. Give him my love and tell him that if he don't want a hole in his old Bread Basket he had Better write to me. I Suppose Lots' Babies grow right Smart Lord how I will make them cry when I come home! I hope they ain't named the youngest one Laura for of all names I ever heard that is the meanest. But I guess I have written enough nonsense for this time give my love to Lot and Charley Mattoon and Wife and Frank Mattoon and all the rest of the folks. So I will close for this time and wish you pleasant Dreams Dear Sister.

Yours with much love from your Brother John,

J E Mattoon

On first examination it appears that not much of anything was going on at Fort Collins at the time. It is possible that letters containing more detail have been lost. Or perhaps John was purposely omitting the details of his days on the Platte as the daily routine of camp life had become commonplace. It was certainly true that the Plains Indians tended to lie low during the winter months, although as late as 1864 they had conducted a savage winter campaign against Colorado settlers.[54] However there was still a great deal of activity on the numerous trails in the immediate region: guarding the mail, stages and wagon trains, and looking out for a variety of trouble from roving lawless elements.

In the aftermath of a few letters containing some potentially tall tales from John, it appears that Annie Mattoon Stone (perhaps just to get even) got into the act as well for there is no record of any gold mine in the vicinity of Canaan, NY. Restless in camp, in a now familiar phrasing John exhibited an interest in adventure, such as a trip to California. It is of interest that John mentioned his pony, a "small sorrel and he can run anything in camp". It could have been an Indian pony and if so it would have been highly prized by the cavalry and difficult to acquire. Thoughts of days gone by with apples, some hard cider, and a good chew of tobacco with Horace Bristol (Charlotte's husband) crop up as well. There is no doubt that John missed seeing his nieces and nephews growing up – and playfully tormenting them. "I Suppose Lots Babies grow right Smart Lord how I will make them cry when I come home." Adding to that jibe, John made sure once again that everyone knew how he felt about the name "Laura." Additionally, John seemed excited at the news that his trusted advisor and elder brother Charley Mattoon, out of the Army for about a year, was a newly married man. Charley wed Alice West in the fall of 1865. They eventually moved to Frederick, Maryland where they raised seven children.

The last extant letter posted by John Mattoon is dated February 22, 1866. Mail service to and from the forts around the Platte was extremely slow in the winter. John had time on his hands as winter had not left the Plains, and "no news of any importance to write" so he uncharacteristically copied a poem that must have hit a personal nerve and addressed it to his beloved sister Annie.

Camp Collins Col. TY
Feb 22nd 1866

Dear Sister,

Your kind and welcome letter was received last night and I was very glad to get another letter from home as it has been a long time since I have received a letter from any one. I am well at present with the exceptions of a bad cold. Thare is no news of any importance to write that I know of. Every thing is dull here but thare is one consollation, we are expected to be mustered out in the spring and then I will have a little trip. Well Annie, I can't think of any more to write so I will write of a song that I have got:

The Soldiers Dream

1st
Our bugles rang twice and the night clouds had lowered
The sentinell stars set their watch in the sky
Thousands had sunk to the ground overpowered
The weary to rest and the wounded to die
As reposing that night on my pallet of straw
The wood searing faggot that quartered the slain
In the dead of the night A sweet vision I saw
And twice ere the morning I dreampt it again

2nd
The thought from the battle fields dreadful affray
Far far had I romed on my desolate track
Twas autumn and sunshine arose on the way
To the home of my Father that welcomed me back
I flew to the pleasant fields traversed so oft
In lifes morning march when my bosom was young
I heard my own mountain goats bleating
I know the sweet song which the corn reapers sung

3rd
They pledge me the wine cup and fondly I swore
My home and my weeping friends never to part
My little ones kissed me a thousand time ore
And my wife wept aloud in the fullness of heart
O stay with us stay thou art weary and worn
And fain was the war broken soldier to stay
But sorrows return with the dawning of morn
And with it my dreamings are melted away

John E Mattoon

Strangely, this romantic poem is by the Scottish poet Thomas Campbell (1777–1844) who wrote it around 1800, when Campbell visited Germany. There he saw the evidence of recent warfare, including an Austrian cavalry charge at Ratisbon, the site of the Napoleonic battle fought at Hohenlinden in December 1800, and, when sailing home, the Danish batteries and the British fleet which took part in the battle of Copenhagen. These sights inspired his martial poems.[55] *The Soldier's Dream* was part of a large corpus of work that gained Campbell great fame in his lifetime and was subsequently revived during the Crimean War, long after Campbell's death in 1844. The poem continued to be quite popular, and was put to music in 1850.[56] How John came to find this poem is not a huge mystery. Victorianism and Romanticism often went hand in hand. Campbell's verses were very likely to have been printed in one of the more accessible newspapers or periodicals like the *Atlantic* or *Harper's Weekly* or perhaps one of the "soldier papers" which often had a section devoted to poetry.[57]

Of further interest is the fact that the poem originally began with the words "Our bugles *sang truce*, for the night-cloud had lower'd." "Twice" was substituted for "truce" in Civil War period publications, totally changing the original intent of the piece, apparently because it was deemed to be insufficiently martial.

Poetry of the period was optimistic and romantic in spirit and form. It was also intensely personal and much more a part of everyday life than it is now. *Leaves of Grass* by Walt Whitman (1855) was an example of preeminent (and in part scandalous) poetry that helped set the tone in America for a world of dreamy egalitarian democracy. That John Mattoon was enamored enough of this particular poem to send it home is interesting, as it is an indictment of the horrors of war and a dreamt vision of the lure of home and hearth. After all of the posturing in his letters that he wanted to continue his adventures, was John now actually thinking of returning home?

IV.   Spring, 1866

Col. Charles Fitz Simmons became one of the very last brevet volunteer promotions to Brigadier General in April of 1866.[58] The new General was instructed to re-establish and expand a camp midway between Fort Halleck and Fort Collins, on the Overland Stage route, named Fort Wardwell (a year later to be renamed Fort Morgan, Wyoming and the site of present-day Fort Morgan, Colorado). Detachments of the 21st manned the Fort until the early summer.

It was common in the period for newspapers to enlist the help of columnists who would write under pseudonyms. "Snoggs" is a case in point. Almost certainly a junior or noncommissioned officer of the 21st New York Cavalry, on May 15, Snoggs related some recent happenings at Fort Wardwell. "This usually dull post is the scene today of a very interesting and exciting ceremony. A handsome pole which for some weeks has been in the process of formation has been elevated to the perpendicular, and for the first time the Stars and Stripes wave o'er our adobe barracks. The pole was raised by ropes and shears, both manned by the sturdy muscle of the Empire State." Snoggs went on to relate: "Major Chas. G. Otis of the 21st New York Cavalry designed this pole . . . [and] having been raised, the command was paraded and the cannons manned at 2 p.m . . . thirty seven guns were fired, one for each state, not forgetting the one we are stationed in." A beer barrel was tapped and "the thing passed off pleasantly."[59]

The latest rumor from Washington was that the Griswold Lights were to be mustered out in June, with most of the men to be paid off at Denver, and finally A Company to be presented at Fort Leavenworth. Denver shopkeepers such as Anker's One Price Store and Peabody and Bros. listed clothing, hats, boots and "fancy lithographed discharges" for sale to the 21st.[60] It is highly likely that John Mattoon's ornate discharge papers[61] came from Anker's or a similar company.

Corresponding with the 21st being mustered out, "In June 1866, the military announced that it would abandon Fort Collins . . . the abandonment of the military fort may have prompted Ben Holladay to sell the Overland Stage Line to Wells Fargo."[62] The railroads were steadily becoming the new haulers and communicators, although the trail continued to be an important highway until 1877 when the Colorado Central Railroad was completed.

The final tally of cavalrymen from the 21st that were actually mustered out at Denver City and Fort Leavenworth in the late summer of 1866 numbered only 309, or a little over seventeen percent of the original total enlistment roll of 1,752 men.[63] At Denver City, Colorado Territory most of the remaining men were finally mustered out and honorably discharged in 1866 as follows: Company B, June 23; Company F, June 26; Company E, July 5 and Company D on July 7. John E. Mattoon was mustered out with Company F. The last company of Civil War enlisted cavalry, Company A, was partially mustered out at Camp Collins and after a three hundred-mile trek. The last seventy men under Capt. Hank Snow were mustered out at Fort Leavenworth Kansas on August 31, 1866 in ninety degree heat.[64] Lt. James Hill sat in front of the barracks along with a U.S. Army paymaster and settled accounts with the men for cash drawn, clothing worn out and other deductions from their mustering out pay.[65] They were the last Civil War volunteer unit in America to be let go – remaining in service one week longer than elements of the 11th Ohio Cavalry.[66]

From the Sand Creek Massacre led by Col. Chivington in the fall of 1864 to early 1867, there existed a critical period for settler's expansion of control in Colorado and Western Dakota Territory. The 21st New York Cavalry regiment fought hardly at all with the Cheyenne or Sioux. They did however safeguard passage on the important Overland Stage route from Denver City, Colorado to Laramie, Wyoming and in so doing helped to protect settlers and communications while advancing the steady migration of people from east to west.

Notes

1.   Reed, 258
2.   Ibid., 259
3.   Ibid.
4.   *Troy New York Daily Times*, (July 30, 1865), 3 Col. 3
5.   Bonnell, 308
6.   *Draper Letter*, (May 30, 1906), Collection of the Author
7.   Bonnell, 188
8.   Ibid., 189
9.   Ibid.
10.   Ibid.
11.   Reed, 259
12.   Ibid., 260
13.   Author's estimates using data from *Civil War Database*; and Bonnell, *Appendix D*, "Roster of the 21st New York Cavalry", 211–342
14.   Reed, 260
15.   Bonnell, 190
16.   Reed, 253-5
17.   Richard N. Ellis. "Volunteer Soldiers in the West." in *Journal of Military Affairs*, (Vol. 34, No. 2, Apr., 1970), 53
18.   Mitchell, 158
19.   Reed, 260
20.   Ibid., 261
21.   Ibid., 262
22.   Ibid., 192
23.   Ellis, *Volunteer Soldiers*, 55
24.   Ibid., 54
25.   Bonnell, 191
26.   Ibid., 193; Reed 263
27.   My own computations, seconded by Bonnell, 193
28.   Garrison, 291
29.   Reed, 263
30.   Fort Collins Public Library, *Local History Archive*, "Fort Collins History and Architecture". Accessed May 21, 2006. Online at: http://library.ci.fort-collins.co.us/local_history/Topics/contexts/colorado.htm. 3
31.   Ibid., "Old Fort Site, 1866"
32.   Reed, 252
33.   Schultz, 153
34.   Ibid.
35.   Editorial, *Rocky Mountain News*. (Nov. 27, 1865), 1 Col. 1
36.   Richard N. Ellis. *General Pope and United States Indian Policy*. (Albequerque, NM: University of New Mexico Press, 1970), 239

37.   Editorial, *Rocky Mountain News*. (Nov. 27, 1865), 1 Col. 1
38.   *Rocky Mountain News*, (July 7, 1865), 2 Col. 1
39.   Ibid., (September 22, 1865), 1 Col. 2
40.   Bonnell, 194
41.   *Rocky Mountain News*, (June 11, 1866), 2 Col. 1
42.   Kenneth Jensen, "Overland Trail Leaves its Mark", *North Forty News*, LaPorte,
        CO: Wise River Companies Inc. (June 2004) Accessed in September of 2006
        at http://www.northfortynews.com/Archive/A200406photoOverlandTrail.htm,
        1
43.   Frank A. Root, *The Overland Stage to California*, (Topeka, Kansas: W.Y.
        Morgan, 1901) 360
44.   Ibid., 195
45.   Wooster, 113
46.   Reed, 266
47.   Mattoon, *Mattoon Family Genealogy*, 23
48.   John E. Mattoon to Charlotte Mattoon Bristol, *Mattoon Letters*, (April 25,
        1864)
49.   Reed, 266
50.   D. O. Wilhelm. *City of Denver Business Directory, 1866*. Denver, (Self-
        Published: 1866). Collection of Colorado State Archives, Denver.
51.   William Hepworth Dixon. *New America*. (Philadelphia: J. B. Lippincott & Co.,
        1867) 46
52.   *Rocky Mountain News*, (January 3, 1866), 4 Col. 1
53.   Reed, 267 cit. *Rochester Daily Democrat*, (January 24, 1866), 4 Col. 1
54.   Smith, 218-20
55.   Scottish Library Association. *Discovering Scottish Writers*. Accessed on
        9/10/2006. Online at http://www.slainte.org.uk/scotauth/campbdsw.htm, 1
56.   Betty T. Bennett. *British War Poetry in the Age of Romanticism; 1793 – 1815*.
        (London: 1976) 17
57.   Wiley, 182
58.   Reed, 269
59.   *Rocky Mountain News*, (May 15, 1866), 1 Col. 1
60.   Ibid., (June 23, 1866), 4 Col. 1
61.   John E. Mattoon *Discharge Papers*. Collection of R. Bruce Donald, Avon, CT.
62.   Jensen, 1
63.   Reed, 300, along with accompanying data at *Civil War Database*, online at
        http://www.civilwardata.com/active/hdsquery.dll?Muster?a=1308&b=U&c=&d
        =6&e=1739&f=20, accessed December, 2006.
64.   Reed, 271
65.   Ibid., xvii
66.   Bonnell, 212

CHAPTER SIX

I.   Home Again

What of the continued journeys of John E. Mattoon? Colorado was a vibrant, growing, and still quite dangerous place in 1866. But many veterans of the 21st chose to stay, contributing to the growth of the area. It was certainly an exciting place, even if the initial pioneer days were about at an end. There was land and opportunity in abundance for those that wanted to work hard and carve out a new life.

But John chose to return to Canaan. He apparently shelved his plans to continue in the Army or Navy or to travel to California, though it is possible he took a short trip to the Golden State or around other western states or territories. It must have taken him at least a few weeks to get home to New York State from Denver City so he may have had a few adventures on the way.

It is a bit puzzling that after making sure his relatives knew from his letters that he would be seeking more adventure away from home that John returned to Columbia County anyway. However there were quite a few very good reasons to return. He had a substantial sum of money in his pocket from his discharge, certainly well over $100 plus any pay in arrears. The temptation to use it up on travel must have clashed with the more conservative goal of setting up a home and having seed capital for the eventual purchase of land. There can also be no question that he had a deep affection for the majority of his family and was very desirous of seeing them again, particularly all of the nieces and nephews that he had never met. Yet another compelling argument for returning was the economics of farming. Agriculture, not the newly booming industrial sector, was still the largest economic factor in the Northeast, and farmers fared much better in terms of their income during the war than did wage earners employed in manufacturing.[1]

The postwar economy still relied heavily on the agricultural sector which continued to be propped up by extensive tariffs designed to keep commodity prices high. Balancing these issues was an immediate nationwide drop in prices for grain as demand from the war dwindled away. However this affected New York less than most states. It was the most heavily industrialized state in the Union and needed a great deal of food for its new class of wage earners. This demand kept farmers in New York in better shape than many who had left for the Mid-West.

Finally, there was a very real element of mental healing that must be addressed. Three out of four service-age men fought in the war nationally. Service in the Union Army for the common soldier was hard at best and there was an element of lawlessness and uncertainty that permeated the atmosphere. John was no paragon of moral rectitude by any means. The extent of John Mattoon's transgressions will never be known because apart from his own accounts, he was never mentioned in the Official Record nor is there any black mark on his service record. It can be posited that the final step to manhood for John Mattoon was to forsake the wildness he participated in with the 21st New York Cavalry and embrace family and community once again.

It is certainly true that in some form or another, John and his compatriot veterans all needed to reach equilibrium in a non-martial society within the relative quiet and support of their families and communities. Most men didn't want to celebrate the end of the war for very long; they just wanted to forget it and get on with life. In fact, it wasn't until decades later when memories had finally faded that the glorifying of the Civil War took place with the memorial-building boom and the establishment of huge fraternal organizations such as the Grand Army of the Republic.

Whatever occurred after he was mustered out on June 26, 1866, it seems certain John made his way home fairly quickly to the life that he knew so well and made up for lost time. A year later on June 2, 1867 he married his brother-in-law Charlie Haight's younger sister Anna. They initially resided in Canaan Four Corners and John once again became that thing he had almost desperately been avoiding for three long years: a farmer. The 1870 United States Census shows the family living in nearby New Lebanon, New York by then and having two boys, Horace B. aged two, and Lewis, an infant. John is listed as a "farm laborer." The family was still in New Lebanon in 1880, but the Census now listed John as a propertied farmer. At that point John and Anna had six children: Horace, twelve, Lewis, ten, Mabel, eight, John E., six, Samuel, three, and Bessie, aged one.[2] Anna Margaret Mattoon was born on October 1, 1883. Three years later in 1886, John Elbert Junior and his sister Bessie both died in unknown circumstances, aged thirteen and eight. Anna Mattoon, perhaps in an effort to replace them, kept at the family and at forty-two years of age in 1889 had Milford C., and again at forty-five in 1892, had her last child, John Elbert II.

In his later years John Mattoon was a valued officer of the Grand Army of the Republic, General Logan Post no. 539, in Chatham, New York. He died on December 23, 1918 at the age of seventy two, possibly due to the influenza pandemic of that year.[3] His beloved wife Anna lived to ninety three years of age passing away in May of 1940.

II.   From Reluctant Farmer to Patriot

John Mattoon experienced a patriotic awakening during his service in the Civil War. The 1860s in Victorian America were a period of highly idealistic rhetoric that more often than not was believed and acted upon by common citizens. John was initially not much swayed by such rhetoric or morality. He knew about the savagery of the war from the reports of his brother Charley and other friends. In 1863 John was battling "war fever", which for him was primarily a lust for adventure mixed with a very real need to leave the drudgery of farming and prove himself so as to garner family (and to a lesser extent public) affirmation. The sense of duty he formed later on was not at all in early evidence. There were no indications from John that the two hugely motivating moral ideologies of that time, religion and the abolition of slavery, had any bearing on his decisions. Additionally, most historians of the Civil War have demonstrated that the late volunteers of 1863 and 1864, many of them lured by bounties into Union blue, were of poor quality and not particularly well-motivated either politically or patriotically. But the personal development of John Mattoon into a man of conviction over almost three years of war necessitates a reassessment of those ideas.

In December of 1863 John E. Mattoon made the decision to go to war. It patently was not a political or moral decision. Adventure away from home and the aforementioned need for community and particularly family approbation, along with a perhaps a nascent component of "duty" provided the individual impetus. The specter of the draft hanging over his head and the lure of the bounty money finally pushed him forward.

Brother Charley Mattoon, already a veteran of much bloody action, wrote to John from Tennessee on March 26, 1864 and gave guidance on what one's duty to country really meant in just six words: "I am rite to serve here". Upon entering service and swimming in bounty money John could have deserted in the first six months like six percent of the entire Regiment did.[4] Dismounted after the battle of New Market and on detached duty, he could easily have deserted, but didn't. John Mattoon was showing a tendency toward performing what he felt was his "duty".

By September of 1864 John's letters indicate that he believed that his family knew that he had met and perhaps exceeded expectations as a citizen soldier, yet he received from them no explicit reassurances. In a lather of self-pity he penned a letter on September 13, 1864. This is the first time that John mentioned "for my country" in any letter. John Mattoon had an awakening of patriotism and nationalism, as he directly linked the welfare of his family and community to the war effort. From whatever source, John had come to believe that he must serve his country.

John wrote to his family of his willingness to die for his beliefs. Much of his flowery Victorian idiom seems out of place or risible now, but it was nothing of the kind in 1860s America. On October 18, 1864 he wrote: "Home is where the heart is, is the old saying and my heart is in the Army and if by falling, [my] life would serve my Country, they should have it a dozen times."⁵ The language was even more heartfelt and sentimental than before as he explained to his dear sister Annie that he now understood that his values were rooted in his love of home. That love and the desire to protect his home from harm and change meant transferring that love to the Army and the job at hand: service to his country.

Because John Mattoon's advancement to manhood and his motivation to stay the course after the novelty of war had worn off were predicated on what he himself experienced at that time, he was surely a product of a unique and special blend of social, political and military history. Military historians might find that John's letters lend some credence to the idea of "unit cohesion," the bonding of Civil War soldiers into surrogate families that demanded defending on the field. Yet John's best friends seemed to remain the friends from home that served with him. Having good senior officers in the 21st who were worthy of respect also may have been important to him. But he never categorized any officer positively or negatively in his letters. So in the case of John E. Mattoon these motivations can only be seen as secondary in nature.

His insular small-town farming culture did, however, provide a substantial social framework that included elements of motivation. John's love of his home and family shines through in many of the letters. It also provides a glimpse into one motivation: reputation. He certainly sought to cultivate a persona that would show his family and his neighbors (and some of his detractors like his brother and sister-in-law George and Mary Mattoon) that he had become a strong, hard fighting man. No longer a boy, he truly had come of age under fire.

Politically, he was a War Democrat in a Republican-led war. His brand of political ideology and culture might seem to point him away from the prosecution of the war, but an overpowering love of the Union and what it stood for (to him) kept him in the fight. Liberty and democracy were at stake, and John understood that the act of defending those ideals was tantamount to defending home and hearth and not just in a symbolic sense. Emancipation from slavery for Southern blacks was never part of John's understanding of "liberty."

These pieces of the motivational puzzle may partly explain how John Mattoon could have progressed from a disaffected farm boy to a duty-bound professional soldier who would painstakingly transcribe a Romantic poem. But is there a broader explanation? Historian James McPherson ascribes much importance to the broad category of "ideology" as the critical motivation of Civil War soldiers. Gerald Linderman, another social historian, has argued in *Embattled Courage* (1987) that "courage" supported by kindred Victorian ideals of masculinity and godliness, duty, honor and knightliness, *not* political ideology, motivated soldiers to fight. Linderman contends that typically "courage" was ground down by the war as romantic images were steadily shattered. Once again John Mattoon does not fit these broad molds.

John never went to war with any romantic images in his mind. By the winter of 1863–64 such noble thoughts were few and far between in the words he wrote home. Initially, all John wanted were the bounty payments, some time away from the drudgery of farming and the prospect of adventure. The conviction that there was a larger purpose came later. It is not farfetched to imagine John Mattoon later in life, when asked about his impressive courage on the battlefield or his continued service when so many had deserted, replying while spitting out some tobacco near (or on) your shoe; "Courage was common as dirt, the hard part was remembering your duty."

John Elbert Mattoon eventually came to believe in his heart that duty was a moral obligation that entailed helping to defend the Union that embodied both his and his family's freedoms. By John's definition, desertion was dishonorable. This is certainly an ideological construct, but in a more homespun, personal, and workmanlike form. This is the tone of many of the early regimental histories written by Civil War participants themselves up to around the period of the First World War, by which time they were dying off at a rapid rate. It took Bell Wiley's first descriptions of the common soldier in *Life of Johnny Reb* (1943) and *Life of Billy Yank* (1952) to push the social history of the common soldier into the public consciousness. These were real men, tough and hardened by today's standards, and many were very rough around the edges indeed.

In the midst of a national conflagration in which over 200,000 men died in battle and over twice that from disease, John E. Mattoon lifted himself by the bootstraps and grew up. His awareness of his duty and his own worth was never voiced more succinctly than in a letter to Annie in March of 1865:

> Often while I sit on my horse all alone I think of you dear Sister and of my friends at home. I long to see you all again but my country before my friends.[6]

Notes

1. Roger L. Ransom, "The Economic Consequences of the American Civil War", in *The Political Economy of War and Peace*, edited by M. Wolfson, Norwell, MA: Kluwer Academic Publishers, 1998. 256–64

2. United States Federal Census. *Town of New Lebanon, Columbia County, State of New York.* (June 25,1870), 6; (June 6,1880), 24

3. I have early 1900's ephemera from the GAR lodge in close-by Chatham, NY indicating John as a past officer. John is buried with his family in Canaan

Cemetery in the town of Canaan, Columbia County, NY., West half of lot #1; Plot #12.
4.   Reed, "Table Seven", 300
5.   John E. Mattoon to Annie Mattoon Stone, *Mattoon Letters*, (October 18, 1864)
6.   John E. Mattoon to Annie Mattoon Stone, *Mattoon Letters*, (March 28, 1865)

BIBLIOGRAPHY

I.　　Unpublished Primary Sources

John E. Mattoon Letters. Collection of R. Bruce Donald, Avon, CT.

John E. Mattoon Ephemera. Misc. Photographs. Pension Bill. Discharge Papers. Collection of R. Bruce Donald, Avon, CT.

William Tibbits Family Papers. (1837–1880). Colonel, 21st New York Cavalry. Record Group KM 13256; Boxes 141, 142, and 143. New York State Archives, Albany, NY.

Richard Arthur Letters. *1863–1870. Auburn University Special Collections & Archives Department, RG 507.*

II.　　Published Primary Sources

Ashby, Thomas A. *The Valley Campaigns, Being the Reminiscences of a Non-combatant while between the Lines in the Shenandoah Valley during the War of the States.* New York: Neale, 1914.

Biddle, Ellen McGowan. *Reminiscences of a Soldier's Wife.* Philadelphia: J.B. Lippincott, 1907, reprint Mechanicsburg, PA: Stackpole Books, 2002.

Custer, Elizabeth B. *Tenting on the Plains: With General Custer from the Potomac to the Western Frontier.* 1887, Reprint: New York: Narrative Press, 2003.

Dixon, William Hepworth. *New America.* Philadelphia: J. B. Lippincott & Co., 1867.

Gardner, Charles. *Three Years in the Cavalry.* Tucson, AZ: Ada Friddell and A Plus Printing, 1909, reprint 1998.

Gilmor, Harry. *Four Years in the Saddle.* New York: Harper and Brothers, 1866.

Glazier, Capt. Willard. *Three Years in the Federal Cavalry.* New York: R. H. Ferguson & Company, 1874.

Howbert, Irving. *Memories of a Lifetime in the Pike's Peak Region.* New York: G.P. Putnam's Sons, 1925.

Mosby, John S. and Russell, Charles, W. (ed.) *The Memoirs of Colonel John S. Mosby.* Boston: Little, Brown & Co. 1917.

Utley, Robert M., (ed) *Life in Custer's Cavalry; Diaries and Letters of Albert and Jennie Barnitz, 1867–1868.* New Haven and London: Yale University Press, 1977.

Sanford, Mollie Dorsey. *Mollie: The Journal of Mollie Dorsey Sanford in Nebraska and Colorado Territories, 1857–1866.* Lincoln: The University of Nebraska Press, 1959.

Springer, Charles H. (Cooling, B.F. III, ed.) *Soldiering in Sioux Country; 1865.* San Diego: Frontier Heritage Press, 1971.

Taylor, James E. *With Sheridan Up the Shenandoah Valley in 1864.* Western Reserve Historical Society. Cleveland: Morningside House, Inc. 1989.

Thorndike, Rachel Sherman. *The Sherman Letters: Correspondence Between General Sherman and Senator Sherman from 1837 to 1891.* New York: DeCapo Press, 1969.

Wilhelm, D. O. *City of Denver Business Directory, 1866.* Denver, CO: 1866.

Wittenberg, Eric J. *We Have It Damn Hard Out Here: The Civil War Letters of Sergeant Thomas W. Smith, 6th Pennsylvania Cavalry.* Kent, OH: Kent State University Press, 1999.

III.   Newspapers and Periodicals

Leavenworth Kansas Times. Leavenworth, KS. 1864–1866.

Rocky Mountain News. Denver City, Colorado Territory. 1864–1866.

Daily Times. Troy, NY. 1862–1866.

Daily Democrat. Rochester, NY. 1862–1867.

Kenneth Jensen, "Overland Trail Leaves its Mark", *North Forty News*, LaPorte, CO: Wise River Companies Inc., June 2004, Accessed Sep. 2006 at http://www.northfortynews.com/Archive/A200406photoOverlandTrail.htm.

IV.   Military, State, and Federal Records

Cooke, Philip, Maj. *Cavalry Tactics and Regulation Instructions for the Instruction, Formation and Movements of the Horse Army.* Washington, DC: War Dept. of the United States of America, 1861.

Military Service Record of John E. Mattoon. New York State Archives, Albany, NY. 1386-7.

Provost Marshal General United States War Dept. *Report of the Provost Marshal General.* Washington, DC: GPO, 1866.

"Reply of Governor Evans, of the Territory of Colorado. To that Part Referring to Him, of the Report of the Committee on the Conduct of the War, headed 'Massacre of Cheyenne Indians'." *Colorado Governor 1862–1865*, Denver: 1865.

Report of the Adjutant General. New York State Archives, Albany, NY: Argus, Vol. V, 1895.

U.S. Senate, 38th Congress. "Massacre of the Cheyenne Indians," *Report of the Joint Committee on the Conduct of the War.* Washington: Government Printing Office, Vol. VI., 1865.

United States Federal Census, *Town of Wethersfield, Hartford County, State of Connecticut.* (25 June 1860), 28.

United States Federal Census, *Town of Wethersfield, Hartford County, State of Connecticut.* (20 July 1870), 42.

United States Federal Census. *Town of New Lebanon, Columbia County, State of New York.* (June 25,1870), 6.

United States Federal Census. *Town of New Lebanon, Columbia County, State of New York.* (June 6,1880), 24.

V. Published Secondary Sources

Barton, Michael, and Logue, Larry M. (eds.) *The Civil War Soldier: A Historical Reader.* New York, London: NYU Press, 2002.

Bennett, Betty T. *British War Poetry in the Age of Romanticism; 1793–1815.* London: 1976.

Billings, John D. *Hardtack and Coffee; or The Unwritten Story of Army Life.* Lincoln: University of Nebraska Press, 1993.

Boatner, Mark M. *The Civil War Dictionary.* New York: David McKay Co. Inc., 1959.

Bonnell, John C. Jr. *Sabres in the Shenandoah: The 21st New York Cavalry: 1863–1866.* Shippensburg, PA: White Mane Publishing, 1996.

Brown, Dee A. *The National Historical Society's The Images of War 1861–1865*, "Fighting for Time" Vol. IV. New York: Doubleday & Co., 1983.

Chanal, Francois Victor Adolphe de. *The American Army in the War of Secession.* Ft. Leavenworth, KS: Spooner, 1894.

Colton, Ray C. *The Civil War in the Western Territories.* Norman: The University of Oklahoma Press, 1959.

Commager, Henry Steele. (ed.) *The Blue and The Grey.* New York: Fairfax Press, 1982.

Ellis, Capt. Franklin, *History of Columbia County, New York.* Philadelphia, PA: Everts & Ensign, 1878.

Faust, Patricia L. (ed.). *Historical Times Encyclopedia of the Civil War.* New York: Harper & Row, 1st edition, 1986.

Foner, Eric. *Reconstruction: America's Unfinished Revolution 1863–1877.* New York: Harper & Row 1988; Reprint HarperCollins, Perennial Classics, 2002.

Foner, Jack D. *The United States Soldier Between Two Wars: Army Life and Reforms, 1865–1898.* New York: Humanities Press, 1970.

Fox, William F. *Regimental Losses in the American Civil War 1861–1865.* Albany, NY: Albany Publishing Company, 1889.

Frank, Joseph Allan. *With Ballot and Bayonet: The Political Socialization of American Civil War Soldiers.* Athens: University of Georgia Press, 1998.

Frazer, Robert W. *Forts of the West; Military Forts and Presidios and Posts Commonly Called Forts West of the Mississippi River to 1898.* Norman: University of Oklahoma Press, 2nd Ed. 1972.

French, J. H. *Gazetteer of New York.* Syracuse, NY: R. P. Smith Co., 1860.

Gallagher, Gary. *Struggle for the Shenandoah: Essays on the 1864 Valley Campaign.* Kent, OH: Ohio State Press, 1991.

Garrison, Webb. *Mutiny in the Civil War.* Shippensburg, PA: White Mane Publishing, 2001.

Grinnell, George Bird. *The Fighting Cheyennes.* Norman: University of Oklahoma Press, 1915.

Heitman, Francis B. *Historical Register and Dictionary of the United States Army.* Vol. II. Washington, DC: GPO 1903.

Historical Data Systems, Inc. *"21st New York Cavalry Regimental Dynamics",* Accessed September 2006. American Civil War Database at http://www.civilwardata.com.

Holzer, Harold, editor. *The Union Preserved: A Guide to Civil War Records in the New York State Archives.* NY: New York State Partnership Trust, 1999.

Linderman, Gerald F. *Embattled Courage: The Experience of Combat in the American Civil War.* New York: Free Press, 1987.

Livermore, Thomas L. *Numbers & Losses in the Civil War in America, 1861–65.* Bloomington, Indiana: UP, 1957.

Lonn, Ella. *Desertion During the Civil War.* NY: Century Press, 1928. Reprint: Lincoln, NB: University of Nebraska Press, 1998.

Mattoon, Lillian G., and Mattoon, Donald P. (eds.) *Genealogy of the Descendants of Philip Mattoon, of Deerfield Massachusetts.* Littleton, NH: Courier Printing Co. 1965.

McPherson, James M. *For Cause and Comrades: Why Men Fought in the Civil War.* New York: Oxford University Press, 1997.

McPherson, James M. and Cooper, William J. Jr. (eds.) *Writing the Civil War: The Quest to Understand.* Columbia: University of South Carolina Press, 1998.

Mitchell, Reid. *The Vacant Chair: The Northern Soldier Leaves Home.* Oxford: Oxford University Press, 1993.

Munden, Kenneth W., and Henry Putney Beers. *The Union: A Guide to Federal Archives Relating to the Civil War.* National Archives and Records Administration. 1962. Reprint, 1986.

Nicholas, David. *Lincoln and the Indians: Civil War Policy and Politics.* 1978, Reprint: Urbana and Chicago, IL: University of Illinois Press, 2000.

Ovies, Adolfo. *Crossed Sabers: General George Armstrong Custer And The Shenandoah Valley Campaign.* New York: Author House, 2005.

Phisterer, Frederick. *Statistical Record of the Armies of the United States.* New York: Scribner, 1883.

Phisterer, Frederick. *New York in the War of the Rebellion*, 3rd ed. Albany, NY: J. B. Lyon Company, 1912.

Preston, Noble Delance. *History of the Tenth Regiment of Cavalry, New York State Volunteers, August, 1861, to August, 1865.* New York: D. Appleton and Co., 1892.

Ransom, Roger L. "The Economic Consequences of the American Civil War." In *The Political Economy of War and Peace.* Wolfson. M., (ed.), Norwell, MA: Kluwer Academic Publishers, 1998.

Rickey, Don Jr. *Forty Miles A Day On Beans And Hay; The Enlisted Soldier Fighting the Indian Wars.* Norman: University of Oklahoma Press, 1963.

Reed, Thomas James. *Tibbits' Boys: A History of the 21st New York Cavalry.* Lanham, MD: University Press of America, 1997.

Robertson, James I. *Soldiers Blue and Gray.* Columbia: University of South Carolina Press, 1988.

Root, Frank A., and Connelley, William E. *The Overland Stage to California.* Topeka, Kansas: W. Y. Morgan, 1901. Reproduced online and accessed January 19, 2006.http://www.rootsweb.com/~neresour/OLLibrary/OLStage/olsp0161.htm.

Sargent, A. Dean. *Grand Army of the Republic: Civil War Veterans, Department of Massachusetts, 1866 to 1947.* Bowie, Md.: Heritage Books, 2002.

Schultz, Duane P. *Month of the Freezing Moon: The Sand Creek Massacre, November 1864.* New York: St. Martin's Press, 1990.

Scottish Library Association. "Discovering Scottish Writers". Accessed online, September 2006. http://www.slainte.org.uk/scotauth/ campbdsw.htm.

Shannon, Fred Albert. *The Organization and Administration of the Union Army 1861–1865.* 2 vols. Cleveland: Arthur H. Clarke & Co. 1928.

Service, Robert. "The Quitter" in *The Best of Robert Service.* New York: Dodd, Mead & Co., 1940.

Silbey, Joel H. *A Respectable Minority: The Democratic Party in the Civil War Era: 1860–1868.* New York: W. W. Norton and Co. 1977.

Smith, Duane A. *The Birth of Colorado: A Civil War Perspective.* Norman: University of Oklahoma Press, 1989.

Smith, Sherry L. *The View from Officers Row: Army Perceptions of Western Indians.* Tucson: University of Arizona Press, 1990.

Starr, Stephen Z. *The Union Cavalry in the Civil War; Volume II, the War in the East from Gettysburg to Appomattox.* Baton Rouge and London: Louisiana State University Press, 1981.

Steffen, Randy. *The Horse Soldier 1851–1880: The Frontier, the Mexican War, the Civil War, the Indian Wars.* Vol. 2, Norman: University of Oklahoma, 1992.

Svaldi, David. *Sand Creek and the Rhetoric of Extermination.* Boston: University Press of America, 1989.

Utley, Robert M. *Frontier Regulars: The U.S. Army and the Indian 1866–1891.* New York: Macmillan Publishing Co., 1973.

Utley, Robert M. *The Indian Frontier of the American West, 1846–1890.* Albuquerque: University of New Mexico Press, 1984.

Vinovskis, Maris A. (ed.) *Toward a Social History of the American Civil War.* Cambridge: Cambridge University Press, 1990.

Warner, Ezra J. *Generals in Blue: Lives of the Union Commanders.* Baton Rouge: Louisiana State University Press, 1964.

Wert, Jeffrey D. *Mosby's Rangers.* New York: Simon and Schuster, 1990.

Whitman, Walt. *Complete Poetry and Collected Prose.* Kaplan, Justin (ed.), New York: Literary Classics of the United States, 1982.

Wiley, Bell Irvin. *The Life of Billy Yank, the Common Soldier of the Union.* Indianapolis: Bobbs-Merrill, 1952.

Williams, Mrs. Ellen. *Three Years and a Half in the Army; or, History of the Second Colorados.* New York: Fowler & Wells Company, 1885.

Wooster, Robert. *The Military and United States Indian Policy 1865–1903.* New Haven: Yale University Press, 1988.

Wright, James Edward. *The Politics of Populism: Dissent in Colorado.* New Haven: Yale University Press, 1974.

VI.   Articles and Journals

Chaput, Donald. "Generals, Indian Agents, Politicians: The Doolittle Survey of 1865." *Western Historical Quarterly*, Vol. 3, No. 3 (Jul., 1972) 269-282 City of Fort Collins Colorado, *Old Fort Cultural Survey Project*, "Old Fort Site 1866". Accessed Online on January 16, 2006; http://fcgov.com/historic preservation/pdf/of-dev-maps.pdf

Cowden, Joanna D. "The Politics of Dissent: Civil War Democrats in Connecticut." *New England Quarterly.* Vol. 56. No. 4, (Dec. 1983) 538-54

Danhof, Clarence H. "Farm-Making Costs and the 'Safety Valve': 1850–1860". *Journal of Political Economy*, Vol. 69, No. 3 (Jun. 1941) 317-59

Dudley, Harold. "The Election of 1864". *Mississippi Valley Historical Review*, Vol. 18, No. 4, (Mar. 1932) 500-18

Ellis, Richard N. "Volunteer Soldiers in the West." *Journal of Military Affairs*, Vol. 34, No. 2, (Apr., 1970) 53-56

Frank, Joseph A. "Measuring the Political Articulateness of United States Civil War Soldiers: The Wisconsin Militia." *Journal of Military History*. Vol. 64, No. 1, (Jan, 2000) 53-77

Gray, John S. "Cavalry and Coaches: The Story of Camp and Fort Collins". *Fort Collins Corral of Westerners*. Fort Collins: Old Army Press, No. 1, (1978)

Millbrook, Minnie D. "Mutiny in Texas". Newsletter, *Little Big Horn Assoc.* 21 (Nov., 1987): 8-16

Moore, John H. "Cheyenne Political History, 1820–1894" *Ethnohistory*, Vol. 21, No. 4 (Autumn, 1974) 329-359

Perrigo, Lynn I. "Law and Order in Early Colorado Mining Camps" *Mississippi Valley Historical Review*, Vol. 28, No. 1 (Jun., 1941) 41-62

Robertson, John "Re-enlistment Patterns of Civil War Soldiers" *Journal of Interdisciplinary History*, Vol. 32, Number 1 (Summer 2001) 15-35

Sherman, Caroline B. and Alvord, Henry E., "A New England Boy in the Civil War" *New England Quarterly*, Vol. 5, No. 2 (Apr., 1932) 310-344

Stelter, Gilbert. "The City and Westward Expansion: A Western Case Study." *Western Historical Quarterly*, Vol. 4, No. 2 (Apr., 1973) 187-202

Tegeder, Vincent G. "Lincoln and the Territorial Patronage: The Ascendancy of the Radicals in the West." *Mississippi Valley Historical Review*, Vol. 35, No. 1 (Jun., 1948) 77-90

Williams, T. Harry. "Voters in Blue: The Citizen Soldiers of the Civil War". *Mississippi Valley Historical Review*. Vol 3, No. ¾ (Sept. 1944) 187-204

INDEX

Fort Halleck, Dakota Territory, 86, 93

Fort Kearny, Nebraska Territory, 82, 84

Fort Leavenworth, KS., 80, 82, 83, 94

Fort Wardwell, Colorado Territory, 93

Frederick City, MD., 65, 89

G

Gardner, Charles, (Pvt. Co. A. 1st Maine Cav.), 35, 40

Garrett's Farm, Port Royal, VA., 66, 67

Geisboro Cavalry Depot, Washington, DC., 18, 20, 26
            Camp Stoneman, 18, 20, 22, 26, 27, 28

Gettysburg, VA, (battle), 16

Gilmore, (Brig. Gen. CSA), 29

Gold Rush,

Gordonsville, VA., raid, 51

Graham, James, (Capt. 21st NY Cav.), 29

Grand Army of the Republic, vii, 98

"Grand Review", 70, 71

Grant, Ulysses S. (Lt. Gen. USA) 31, 59, 60

Green Spring Run Station, WV., 44, 45

Griswold, John A., (U.S. Congressman, Troy, NY), 10

Guerrilla(s), 49, 65

H

Haight, Charles "Charley", 5, 7, 8, 16, 55, 57, 87

Halltown, WV., 24, 39, 89

Harpers Ferry, WV., 22, 23, 27, 29, 39, 59

Harris, Cordelia, (Wethersfield, CT), 1, 3, 4, 56

Hogeboom, Peter, (Capt. 21st NY Cav.), 80

Holcomb, Nelson, (Lt. NY 21st Cav.), 48

Holdridge, Edgar, (Pvt. 21st NY Cav.), 28, 29

Holliday, Ben, 86, 87, 94

Homestead Law, 72

Horses, 21, 27, 31, 81, 90, 91

Hunter, David (Maj. Gen. USA), 26, 29, 31

I

Imboden, John D., (Brig. Gen. CSA), 26, 30

Indians, see American Indians

J

Jackson, Andrew, 40

Johnson, Andrew, (President U.S.) 74, 85

Johnson, Bradley T., (Brig. Gen. CSA), 61

K

Kansas Military Units,
            11th Cavalry, 84

Kernstown, VA., battle, 30

L

Lee, Robert E. (Maj. Gen CSA), 16, 61

Lincoln, Abraham, 26, 46, 47, 61, 66

Lomax, Lunsford L., (Maj. Gen. CSA), 48

Lynchburg, VA., 55

M

Mail Call, 42

About the Author

This is Robert "Bruce" Donald's first book although he has written a multitude of documents over many years in the course of a marketing career for Wall Street firms, the CEO of a provider of online content for corporate Web sites, and as an independent business consultant. He has also written monographs, reviews, and short non-fiction stories. A graduate of Middlebury College in Vermont with a degree in Political Science, he also earned a Masters Degree in History from Trinity College in Hartford, Connecticut. He continues to enjoy a life-long interest in history of all kinds, and is a proud Son of the American Revolution. He is an officer or board member for a number of not-for-profit organizations. An avid sportsman, he lives in Connecticut.